教育部哲学社会科学重大攻关项目"汉语国际教育祖
中国文化教材与数据库建设研究"（18JZD01

3

Cultural Code

Wenhua Mima
Zhongguo Wenhua
Jiaocheng

文化密码
中国文化教程
Chinese Culture Course

主编　于小植

编者　于小植　李建新

译者　寇昕瑛

中国教育出版传媒集团
高等教育出版社·北京

图书在版编目（CIP）数据

文化密码：中国文化教程. 3 / 于小植主编；于小
植，李建新编者. -- 北京：高等教育出版社，2023.2
（2025.3 重印）-- ISBN 978-7-04-056733-5

Ⅰ. ①文… Ⅱ. ①于… ②李… Ⅲ. ①中华文化—高
等学校—教材 Ⅳ. ①K203

中国版本图书馆CIP数据核字 (2021) 第162871号

| 策划编辑 | 王　群 | 责任编辑 | 王　群 | 封面设计 | 王　鹏 | 版式设计 | 孙　伟 |
| 责任绘图 | 王　琰 | 插图选配 | 王　群 | 责任校对 | 李　玮 | 责任印制 | 赵　佳 |

出版发行	高等教育出版社	购书热线	010-58581118
社　　址	北京市西城区德外大街 4 号	咨询电话	400-810-0598
邮政编码	100120	网　　址	https://www.hep.com.cn
印　　刷	北京中科印刷有限公司	网上订购	https://mall.hep.com.cn
开　　本	889mm×1194mm 1/16	版　　次	2023 年 2 月第 1 版
印　　张	11.5	印　　次	2025 年 3 月第 2 次印刷
字　　数	238千字	定　　价	68.00 元

本书如有缺页、倒页、脱页等质量问题，请到所购图书销售部门联系调换
版权所有　侵权必究
物 料 号　56733-B0

前　言

尊敬的老师、亲爱的同学：

欢迎使用《文化密码 —— 中国文化教程》！

《文化密码 —— 中国文化教程》是为来华留学生和海外中文学习者编写的以"中国文化"为主题的系列教程，共 6 册，从"零"起步、循序渐进、层递深入，可以满足初级、中级、高级不同中文水平学习者的学习需求。

在编写中，我们注重中国思想文化源流与当代中国的内在联系，以文化知识为主线，以文化因素为隐线，建构了具有选择性而非面面俱到的、具有发展性而非固化不变的、具有开放性而非封闭保守的、具有灵活性而非按部就班的螺旋式文化主题体系，帮助学习者形成对中国文化的系统印象。

本系列教程共 31 个文化主题，分布在 6 册之中，每个文化主题下包含 3 课教学内容。我们格外注重中国文化可供世界分享的价值，因此每册都编排了"中国智慧"主题。

第 1 册	姓名文化、饮食文化、科技文化、旅游文化、汉字文化、中国智慧
第 2 册	地理文化、历史文化、民俗文化、节日文化、文化遗产、中国智慧
第 3 册	城市文化、建筑文化、服饰文化、休闲文化、戏曲文化、中国智慧
第 4 册	茶文化、酒文化、书法文化、绘画文化、儒家文化、中国智慧
第 5 册	制度文化、器物文化、诗歌文化、道家文化、中医文化、中国智慧
第 6 册	文化要义、文化精神、文化交流、墨家文化、佛教文化、中国智慧

本系列教程具有系统性、综合性、可操作性和实践性强的特点，可以使学习者在习得中国文化的过程中由低至高，逐渐具备文化认知能力、文化理解能力、文化讲述能力、文化阐释能力、跨文化比较能力和文化迁移创新能力。为了帮助学习者获得上述能力，每课我们都遵循 8 个教学环节进行设计，分别是：热身活动、课文、生词（含文化词语）、课文理解练习、文化理解练习、课堂文化交际、课后文化实践、文化常识。在每个单元结尾，我们设置了单元自评，帮助学习者及时总结评估。另外，每课我们都提供了二维码，方便学习者扫码使用配套数字资源。

本系列教程对于学习者来说，既是一次语言接触，也是一次文化接触。与以往的文化教程相比，本系列教程的最大特点在于：语言能力提升与文化知识掌握并举；满足学习者对中国文化"知"的需求，同时，使学习者具有流利"说"中国文化的语言能力和跨文化交际能力，以及将来作为文化交流使者传播中国文化的能力。

柳宗元说："夫美不自美，因人而彰。兰亭也，不遭右军，则清湍修竹，芜没于空山矣。"我们希望本系列教程是对中国文化"清湍修竹"的发现、拾英、照亮、创作和生成；我们期待本系列教程可以使学习者对中国文化"一见如故"并与中国文化"长相厮守"；我们期待学习者通过对本系列教程的学习，可以与中国心灵相通、知华友华；我们期待中国文化能对学习者的伦常日用、修齐治平产生积极影响；我们期待学习者将来站在世界的舞台上，能够使中国文化产生更大的"界外之响""化外之力"。

本系列教程是教育部哲学社会科学重大攻关项目"汉语国际教育视野下的中国文化教材与数据库建设研究"（18JZD018）的部分实践成果，入选教育部中外语言交流合作中心的"国际中文教育精品教材 1+2 工程"项目，谨此向教育部对我们的支持和信任致以谢忱。教程的编写团队 30 余人，其中主要编写者 7 人，向团队的辛苦付出致以谢忱。在编写过程中，高等教育出版社的王群、李玮编辑深度参与，提出了许多有价值的建议和意见；美编王琰构图精美；封面设计王鹏与版式设计孙伟匠心独运，向高等教育出版社致以谢忱。

中国文化是一种仰之弥高、钻之弥深的文化，尽管我们焚膏继晷、将勤补拙，但教程中一定存在挂一漏万之处，恳请老师和同学们指正！我们的邮箱是 whmmxljc@163.com。

主编　于小植

2020 年 10 月 10 日

于北京语言大学

Foreword

Dear teachers and students,

Welcome to *Cultural Code: Chinese Culture Course*!

Designed for international students in China and overseas students who are learning Chinese, *Cultural Code: Chinese Culture Course* is a series of courses about Chinese culture. The 6 coursebooks have **step-by-step instructions** that are designed to serve the respective needs of **beginner, intermediate, and advanced level** students.

The purpose of this series is to explore the relationship between the sources of Chinese ideology and the culture of present-day China. With a primary theme of cultural knowledge and a secondary theme of cultural factors, these courses aim to provide a cultural learning spiral that is selective rather than all-encompassing, developmental rather than static and flexible rather than rigid. The ultimate goal is to help students form a systematic impression of Chinese culture.

The 6 coursebooks include 31 cultural themes, with 3 lessons in each theme. We include a "Chinese Wisdom" theme in every coursebook because we value the application of Chinese culture beyond borders.

Coursebook 1	Culture in Names, Culture in Food, Culture in Technology, Culture in Tourism, Culture in Chinese Characters, Chinese Wisdom
Coursebook 2	Culture in Geography, Culture in History, Culture in Customs, Culture in Holidays, Cultural Heritage, Chinese Wisdom
Coursebook 3	Culture in Cities, Culture in Architecture, Culture in Costume, Culture in Leisure, Culture in Chinese Opera, Chinese Wisdom
Coursebook 4	Tea Culture, Wine Culture, Culture in Calligraphy, Culture in Painting, Culture in Confucianism, Chinese Wisdom
Coursebook 5	Institutional Culture, Culture in Objects, Culture in Poetry, Culture in Taoism, Culture in Traditional Chinese Medicine, Chinese Wisdom
Coursebook 6	Essence of Culture, Spirit of Culture, Cultural Communication, Culture in Mohism, Culture in Buddhism, Chinese Wisdom

This series provides highly systematic, comprehensive, accessible and practical learning experiences of Chinese culture. Meanwhile, it allows students to **recognize, comprehend, narrate, interpret, compare and innovatively transfer culture**. To achieve these goals, each lesson is designed with 8 parts: Warm Up, Text, New Words and Expressions (including Cultural Words), Text Comprehension, Cultural Reading Comprehension, Cultural Communication, Cultural Practice and Cultural Knowledge. The

Self-Assessment at the end of every unit acts as a summative evaluation for students. In addition, QR codes are available for every lesson so that you can conveniently access related resources.

This series exposes students to both Chinese language and Chinese culture. Compared to culture coursebooks available, the unique feature of this course is its equal emphasis on language proficiency and cultural knowledge. In "getting to know" Chinese culture, students can gain fluency in "talking about" Chinese culture, develop intercultural communication skills and acquire the potential to promote Chinese culture in the future.

The great poet of Tang Dynasty, Liu Zongyuan, said that "Beauty is never self-granted, but owes its existence to the beholder. Had it not been for Wang Youjun, the clear streams and slender bamboos around the Orchid Pavilion would have been a vain waste on the mountains." Likewise, we hope this series could provide students with a sense of familiarity on their first acquaintance with Chinese culture and the ability to develop Chinese culture into an ever-lasting companionship. We hope that, by studying this series, students could grasp the essence of Chinese spirit and befriend Chinese people. We hope that, Chinese culture could have a positive impact on students' ethics, day-to-day behavior, moral practices and self-cultivation. Eventually, we hope to see students carry Chinese culture beyond borders and increase its global impact.

This series is a part of the research outcomes of the project "Chinese Culture Coursebook and Corpus Construction Research from the Perspective of International Chinese Education" (18JZD018), a Major Project of the Philosophy and Social Sciences of the Ministry of Education. It is also selected into the "International Chinese Education Excellent Textbooks 1+2 Project" of Center for Language Education and Corperation of the Ministry of Education. So we would like to express our gratitude towards the Ministry of Education for its support and trust. We would also like to give special thanks to our writing and editing team with over 30 members, 7 of whom are main writers, as well as the publisher, Higher Education Press. Lastly, we would like to express our appreciation for the valuable advice and suggestions offered by Senior Editor Wang Qun and Li Wei from Higher Education Press. We are deeply grateful for their involvement and precious contribution. We would also like to express our appreciation to Art Editor Wang Yan, Cover Designer Wang Peng and Layout Designer Sun Wei for their elaborate and elegant illustrations and design.

The closer one approaches the core of Chinese culture, the more profound one finds it to be. Despite our best efforts, occasional errors and shortcomings remain inevitable. Any correction and criticism will be sincerely appreciated. Please contact us through email at *whmmxljc@163.com*.

Chief Editor: Yu Xiaozhi
Beijing Language and Culture University
October 10th, 2020

使用说明

  本册教程是《文化密码 —— 中国文化教程》系列的第 3 册，**适用于中级中文水平学习者**。本册有 6 个文化主题单元，分别是：城市文化、建筑文化、服饰文化、休闲文化、戏曲文化和中国智慧。为了使学习者在了解中国文化的同时，提高中文表达能力，本册精选名家名篇，展现生动有趣的中国文化，让学习者掌握地道标准的中文表达。本册教程以语言的交际功能训练为基础，以体演文化教学法为指导，结合听说法、情境法、交际法、任务法等多种教学方法的长处，为学习者提供多角度、多层次的语言练习，以期达到使学习者在语言实践中掌握中国文化的目的。**每课**的建议教学时长为 **2—4 课时**，任课教师可根据学生的具体情况和教学安排酌情调整。需要说明的是：

  一、**课文**不再采用对话体，而是选用经典语篇，且大部分摘自名家名篇，以增强中级学习者的语篇阅读能力和成段表达能力，使其感受中文的语言魅力，体验中国文化之美。

  二、**生词（含文化词语）**包括了本册中首次出现的中文词或词组。为了便于中文学习者理解，生词按照其在课文中的用法进行释义，而非完全按照词典中对词汇的界定出现。为了突出"文化"特色，我们单独列出了文化词语，以便于学习者学习掌握。

  三、**课文理解练习**主要帮助学习者进一步理解课文内容及重要词汇和句型结构。小词库和文化小词库提供了在完成练习中可能需要用到的词语，不要求学习者全部掌握，教师可以根据实际情况，适当增减需要认读学习的词语。

  四、**文化理解练习**是针对每课的文化主题补充的阅读理解练习。小词库和文化小词库可以帮助学习者更好地理解阅读材料，同样不要求学习者全部掌握。

  五、**课堂文化交际**是围绕课文内容的对话练习，建议在课上以双人对话形式开展，旨在复现本课核心文化知识和关键词句，提高学习者的中文交际表达能力。

  六、**课后文化实践**建议作为课后作业，帮助学习者亲身实践、体验中国文化，引导学习者自主思考、发现中国文化的特点以及与学习者母语国文化间的不同。建议教师在每课结束时布置文化实践任务，并在下次课的热身阶段检查学习者的完成情况。

  七、**文化常识**是每课对于文化点的知识性补充，以中英双语呈现。教师可以酌情安排学习者自学，以增进学习者对该文化点的了解。

  八、本册教程配有微课、电子课件（PPT）、MP3 音频等。相关配套资源可扫描书中二维码获取。

Instruction

This is *Coursebook 3* of *Cultural Code: Chinese Culture Course* designed for **intermediate level students of Chinese**. There are 6 units in this coursebook — Culture in Cities, Culture in Architecture, Culture in Costume, Culture in Leisure, Culture in Chinese Opera, and Chinese Wisdom, each dealing with a popular theme in Chinese culture. The classic works of outstanding writers were carefully selected in the Texts to enhance students' oral performance and kindle their interest in studying Chinese culture. This coursebook mainly follows the principles of the performed culture approach, yet meanwhile brings together the advantages of various pedagogical approaches such as the audiolingual method, the situational teaching method, the communicative approach, and the task-based method, etc. The multifaceted and stratified language exercises devised thereon help students to have a solid grasp on Chinese culture. The recommended **teaching hours for each lesson is 2—4 class hours**, but could be adjusted according to students' levels. Of note here are the following:

1. The **Text** no longer adopts dialogues, but instead classic passages most of which are selected from well-known works of famed masters. This allows intermediate learners to enhance their ability on reading texts and paragraph expression where they can experience the charm of Chinese language and the beauty of Chinese culture.

2. **New Words and Expressions (including Cultural Words)** are listed when they are introduced for the first time. In order to facilitate students' better understanding, words are explained as they appear in the Texts rather than they are defined in the dictionary. Meanwhile, **Cultural Words and Expressions** are listed separately to highlight the cultural features and make it easy for students to understand and study.

3. **Text Comprehension** aims to further students' understanding of the text and using essential vocabulary and sentence patterns. **Word Bank** and **Cultural Word Bank** provide extra vocabulary needed to complete exercises, which are not compulsory, and up to teachers' adjustments as appropriate.

4. **Cultural Reading Comprehension** is reading comprehension based on the cultural theme in each unit. The **Word Bank** and **Cultural Word Bank** in this part only aim to facilitate students' understanding of the passages. Therefore, it is not compulsory for students to master them.

5. **Cultural Communication** is the dialogue exercises centred on the content of the Texts. It is recommended that it should be carried out in the form of a two-person dialogue in class. The aim is to recall the core cultural knowledge and the key words and expressions of this lesson in order to improve learners' communication skills.

6. We recommend using **Cultural Practice** as homework. This part provides an opportunity for hands-on experiences of Chinese culture, which can help students actively ponder and discover the characteristics of Chinese culture and become aware of how it differs from their own culture. We recommend that teachers assign this section as homework after each lesson and conduct homework check during **Warm Up** of the next lesson with appropriate focuses.

7. **Culture Knowledge** is an extension to the cultural content in each lesson and is presented in both Chinese and English. Students are encouraged to study this section independently in order to foster an understanding of relevant cultural content covered in each lesson.

8. Students can **scan the QR codes** to view micro-courses, and download PPT slides, MP3 audio and other resources attached to this coursebook.

目录

名字取自《诗经》中"所谓伊人，在水一方"。人如其名，性格恬静、温婉。美籍华裔，会一点儿汉语。22岁。回中国帮爷爷寻找失散多年的朋友。

Song Yiren, 22-year-old American-born Chinese, got her name from a line in *The Book of Odes*, "The fair lady (伊人 Yīrén) I am thinking of is somewhere by the water". The name fits nicely into Yiren's quiet and gentle temperament. She can speak a little Chinese, and has come to China in search of her grandfather's long lost friend.

因为喜欢李小龙，所以自己取名"大龙"。他的英文姓是Durant，后取了中国姓"杜"。美国人，喜欢中国文化，23岁，刚开始学汉语。为人风趣，是宋伊人的男朋友，陪伊人一起来中国。

Dalong (means Big Dragon), 23-year-old American, gave himself this name out of his adoration for kung fu star Bruce Lee (李小龙 Lǐ Xiǎolóng). He adapted his surname Durant to the Chinese Surname Du (杜 Dù). He is humorous and has an interest in Chinese culture, and has just started studying Chinese. He is Song Yiren's boyfriend and has come to China to keep her company.

因为五行缺火，所以父母给她取名字叫"晶"。人如其名，性格活泼，做事果敢。宋伊人的表姐，23岁。

Li Jing, 23-year-old, is Song Yiren's elder cousin. Her parents believed that the "Fire" element was missing from her fate, so named her Jing (晶 Jīng, which is comprised of three 日 rì, the sun). She is outgoing and decisive, just as her name suggests.

名字取自《论语》的"有朋自远方来"。为人诚恳憨厚。李晶的男朋友，23岁。

Wang Youpeng, 23-year-old, is Li Jing's boyfriend. He is honest and has a good nature. He got his name from a line in *The Analects of Confucius*, "I have (有 yǒu) friends (朋 péng) coming from afar".

第一单元
UNIT ❶

城市文化
Culture in Cities

第1课
Lesson 1

Běijīng chéng
北京城

热身活动 Warm Up

1. 说一说你对北京的印象。
2. 你知道北京故宫、天坛和地坛吗？

课文 Text

世界上像北京设计得这么方方正正的城市很少见。因为住惯了这样布局齐整的地方，一去外省，总是迷路转向。瞧，这儿以紫禁城（故宫）为中心，前有

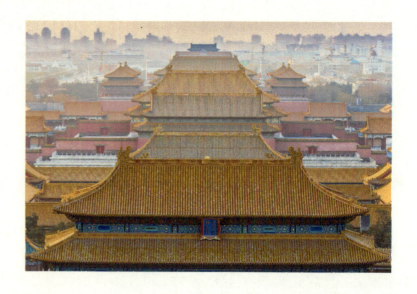

天安门，后有地安门，前后对称；北城有钟、鼓二楼，四面是天、地、日、月坛。街道则有东单西单、南北池子。全城街道就没几条斜的，斜街都特别标明了，有条樱桃斜街，鼓楼旁边儿有个烟袋斜街。胡同呢，有些也挨着个儿编号：从头条、二条一直到十二条，编到十二条，觉得差不多了，就不往下编了，给它叫起名字来，什么香饵胡同呀、石雀胡同呀，都起得十分别致。

（摘编自《布局和街名》，有删改）

生 词 New Words and Expressions

1.	设计	shèjì	design
2.	方方正正	fāngfāng zhèngzhèng	square-shaped
3.	惯	guàn	be used to
4.	布局	bùjú	layout
5.	总是	zǒngshì	always
6.	迷路	mílù	get lost
7.	转向	zhuànxiàng	lose one's sense of direction
8.	瞧	qiáo	look
9.	中心	zhōngxīn	centre
10.	对称	duìchèn	symmetrical

11.	坛	tán	altar
12.	则	zé	so, thus, therefore
13.	池子	chízi	pond
14.	斜	xié	inclining
15.	挨着个儿	āizhe gèr	one by one
16.	编	biān	number, compile
17.	头条	tóu tiáo	(used in *hutong* names) the First *Hutong*
18.	别致	biézhì	unique and elegant

文化词语
Cultural Words

1.	外省	wài shěng	provinces other than where one is
2.	紫禁城	Zǐjìnchéng	the Forbidden City
3.	钟、鼓楼	Zhōng, Gǔ Lóu	Bell Tower and Drum Tower
4.	天、地、日、月坛	Tiān, Dì, Rì, Yuè Tán	Temple of Heaven, Temple of the Earth, Temple of the Sun and Temple of the Moon
5.	樱桃斜街	Yīngtao Xiéjiē	Yingtao Xiejie, Inclining Cherry Street
6.	烟袋斜街	Yāndài Xiéjiē	Yandai Xiejie, Inclining Pipe Street
7.	香饵胡同	Xiāng'ěr Hútòng	Xiang'er *Hutong*, Delicious Bait Hutong
8.	石雀胡同	Shíquè Hútòng	Shique *Hutong*, Stone Sparrow Hutong

课文理解练习 Text Comprehension

 根据课文选一选 Choose the Right Answers Based on the Text

1. 北京城是什么形状的?

A ☐

圆形的

B ☐

正方形的

C ☐

斜的

D ☐

三角形的

2. 鼓楼旁边的是什么?

A ☐ 烟袋斜街 YANDAI XIEJIE

B ☐ 樱桃斜街 YINGTAO XIEJIE

C ☐ 石雀胡同 SHIQUE HUTONG

D ☐ 香饵胡同 XIANGER HUTONG

根据提示说一说 Complete the Sentences Based on the Given Clues

1. 因为住惯了这样布局齐整的地方，一去外省，总是迷路转向。

一……，总是……

❶ 一想到北京城，_____。（整齐的布局）

❷ 一说到世界上设计得方方正正的城市，_____。（北京）

❸ 一提到鼓楼，_____。（烟袋斜街）

❹ 一听到香饵胡同呀、石雀胡同呀，_____。（名字、别致）

2. 这儿以紫禁城（故宫）为中心。

以……为……

❶ 老北京城的设计_____。（方方正正、主）

❷ 天安门和地安门_____，前后对称。（故宫、中心）

❸ 全城街道_____，就没几条斜的。（直的、主）

❹ 胡同呢，有些_____挨着个儿编号：从头条、二条一直到十二条。（数字、名字）

文化理解练习 Cultural Reading Comprehension

 **读一读，想一想** Read and Think

　　我是大龙，今天我读了中国作家汪曾祺的《胡同文化》。汪曾祺在《胡同文化》中写道："北京城像一块大豆腐，四方四正。城里有大街，有胡同。大街、胡同都是正南正北，正东正西。街道是斜的，就特别标明是斜街，如烟袋斜街、杨梅竹斜街。"这些大街和胡同把北京切成一个又一个方块。

1. 中国作家汪曾祺说北京城像什么？

    A 一块饼干   B 一本书   C 一块大豆腐   D 一个手机

2. 北京城的大街、胡同都是什么样的？（多选）

    A 正南正北   B 正东正西   C 歪歪斜斜   D 弯弯曲曲

课堂文化交际 Cultural Communication

 小组活动   Group Activity

选词填空，完成对话。再两人一组练习对话。

对话一 Dialogue 1

> 方方正正的 故宫 天安门 地安门 对称 钟楼 鼓楼 天坛 地坛
> 日坛 月坛

 大龙，你在看什么？

 我在看北京地图呢。

 你觉得北京城设计得怎么样？

 北京城以 _____ 为中心，设计得 _____ 。

 北京城前有 _____ ，后有 _____ ，前后 _____ 。

 是的，北京的北城有 _____ ，四面是 _____ 。

对话二 Dialogue 2

挨着个儿　头条　石雀胡同　樱桃斜街　烟袋斜街

 大龙，你知道北京的胡同怎么编号吗？

 北京的胡同 _____ 编号，从 _____ 、二条一直到十二条。

 你听说过哪些胡同的名字呢？

 我听说过 _____ 和香饵胡同。

 北京的街道大部分是正南正北的，但也有几条斜的街道，你知道吗？

 我知道有条 _____ ，鼓楼旁边儿有个 _____ 。

课后文化实践 Cultural Practice

👤 个人活动 Individual Activity

今天我们在课文中学习了香饵胡同和石雀胡同，北京还有许多有名的胡同，请你到北京的胡同里转一转，或者在网上查一查，下节课给大家介绍一个你最喜欢的胡同吧！

北京的胡同	1.	2.	3.	4.
特点				
最喜欢的胡同				
原因				

胡同 *Hutong*

胡同在北方用为巷道的通称，一般连通两条或多条主干街道，并一直通向居民区的内部。它是交通中不可或缺的一部分。根据道路情况，有种胡同称为"死胡同"。"死胡同"只有一个开口，末端深入居民区，并且在内部中断。北京最有特色的胡同是南锣鼓巷、烟袋斜街、帽儿胡同、国子监街、琉璃厂文化街、金鱼胡同、东交民巷、西交民巷、菊儿胡同和八大胡同。

Hutong generally refers to narrow lanes or alleys connecting major streets in cities and usually leads to residential areas in the northern part of China. An indispensable booster for local mobility, *hutong* usually connects two or more major streets. However, there is the dead *hutong*, which only opens up at one end and breaks off in residential areas. The famous *hutongs* in Beijing are Nan Luogu Xiang (South Gong Lane), Yandai Xiejie (Inclining Pipe Street), Mao'er *Hutong* (Hat *Hutong*), Guozijian Jie (Imperial Academy Street), Liuli Chang Culture Street (Glass Factory Street), Jinyu *Hutong* (Goldfish *Hutong*), Dongjiaomin Xiang (East Jiaomin Alley), Xijiaomin Xiang (West Jiaomin Alley), Ju'er *Hutong* (Chrysanthemum *Hutong*), and Eight Great *Hutongs*.

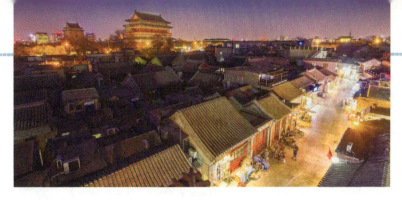

烟袋斜街 Yandai Xiejie (Inclining Pipe Street)

烟袋斜街位于北京什刹海历史文化保护区的核心区内，东起地安门外大街，西邻什刹海前海，为东北西南走向，全长232米，宽5至6米，是北京最古老的商业街之一。烟袋斜街始建于元朝，清末这里主要经营烟具、装裱字画和售卖古玩玉器。目前，烟袋斜街的商业业态有以工艺品、服装服饰为主的零售业和以餐饮、酒吧及经济型酒店为主的住宿餐饮业。由于烟袋斜街的胡同肌理没有改变，基本建筑风格没有改变，并富含历史文化信息和城市记忆，2010年，烟袋斜街被认定为"中国历史文化名街"。

Located in the core of Shichahai Historical and Cultural Preservation Area, Yandai Xiejie (Inclining Pipe Street) is one of the oldest commercial streets in Beijing. Going from the northeast to the southwest, it is 232 metres long and five to six metres wide with its east end on the Di'anmenwai Street and the west end to the Qianhai (Front Sea) of Shichahai. Yandai Xiejie was first built in the Yuan Dynasty. By the end of the Qing Dynasty, it was used as a marketplace for smoking paraphernalia, mounted Chinese calligraphy and painting, antiques, and jade ware. Today, the two pivotal industries in this area are retailing (craft and clothing) and accommodation and catering (such as restaurants, bars, hostels, etc). Undiluted in its *hutong* texture and basic constructional style, Yandai Xiejie was listed as one of "the Chinese Historical and Cultural Streets" for its rich historical and cultural contents as well as urban memory.

02

Shànghǎi de lòngtáng
上海的弄堂

课 文 Text

　　上海的弄堂，条数巨万，纵的、横的、斜的、曲的，如迷魂阵。每届盛夏，大半个都市笼在炎雾中，傍晚日光西射，建筑物构成阴带，人们都坐卧在弄堂里。藤椅、竹榻、帆布床、小板凳，摆得弄堂难于通行，路人却又川流不息。纳凉的芸芸众生时而西瓜，时而凉粉，时而大麦茶绿豆汤和莲子百合红枣汤，暗中又有一层比富炫阔的心态，真富真阔早就庐山避暑了，然而上海人始终在比下有余中忘了比上不足。老太婆衣履端正，轻摇羽扇，曼声叫孙女儿把银耳羹拿出来，要加冰糖，当心倒翻；老头子，上穿讲究的衬衫，下穿笔挺的长裤，乌亮的皮拖鞋十年也不走样，小板凳为桌，一两碟小菜，啜他的法国三星白兰地，消暑祛疫，环顾悠然。

（摘编自《弄堂风光》，有删改）

生 词 New Words and Expressions

1.	纵（的）	zòng(de)	vertical
2.	迷魂阵	míhúnzhèn	maze, labyrinth
3.	届	jiè	when or which
4.	大半个	dà bàn ge	a greater half
5.	都市	dūshì	city
6.	笼	lǒng	cover, enshroud
7.	炎雾	yánwù	summer heat
8.	傍晚	bàngwǎn	dusk
9.	建筑物	jiànzhùwù	building
10.	构成	gòuchéng	form
11.	藤椅	téngyǐ	cane chair
12.	竹榻	zhútà	bamboo couch
13.	帆布床	fānbùchuáng	camp bed
14.	小板凳	xiǎo bǎndèng	small stool
15.	摆	bǎi	lay, display
16.	难于通行	nányú tōngxíng	difficult to go through
17.	川流不息	chuānliú bùxī	ceaselessly move around as a flowing river
18.	纳凉	nàliáng	enjoy the cool in hot weather
19.	时而	shí'ér	once in a while
20.	暗中	ànzhōng	on the sly
21.	比富炫阔	bǐfù xuànkuò	flaunt one's wealth
22.	然而	rán'ér	however
23.	始终	shǐzhōng	from the beginning to the end
24.	羽扇	yǔshàn	feather fan
25.	曼声	mànshēng	drawl
26.	穿	chuān	wear
27.	讲究	jiǎngjiu	refined
28.	衬衫	chènshān	shirt
29.	笔挺	bǐtǐng	trim
30.	长裤	chángkù	trousers
31.	碟	dié	dish
32.	啜	chuò	sip
33.	白兰地	báilándì	brandy
34.	消暑祛疫	xiāoshǔ qūyì	reduce heat and curb diseases
35.	环顾悠然	huángù yōurán	look around leisurely

文化词语
Cultural Words

1. 弄堂	lòngtáng	narrow lane or alley
2. 芸芸众生	yúnyún zhòngshēng	the masses
3. 大麦茶绿豆汤	dàmàichá lǜdòutāng	barley tea and mung bean soup
4. 莲子百合红枣汤	liánzǐ bǎihé hóngzǎo tāng	lotus seed, lily root and Chinese-date soup
5. 比上不足，比下有余	bǐ shàng bùzú, bǐ xià yǒuyú	passable, tolerable
6. 银耳羹	yín'ěrgēng	white fungus soup

课文理解练习 Text Comprehension

根据课文选一选 Choose the Right Answers Based on the Text

1. 每届盛夏，上海大半个都市都笼（罩）在什么中？

A 阴雨

B 大风

C 炎雾

D 晴空

2. 上穿讲究的衬衫，下穿笔挺的长裤，乌亮的皮拖鞋十年也不走样的是谁？

A 上海的男人

B 上海的老头子

C 北京的老太婆

D 北京的老头子

💬 **根据提示说一说** Complete the Sentences Based on the Given Clues

1. 上海的弄堂，条数巨万，纵的、横的、斜的、曲的，**如**迷魂阵。

> ……**如/如同**……（一般）

　①　盛夏的上海笼在炎雾中，_____。（蒸笼）

　②　弄堂里的路人来来往往，_____。（流水）

　③　老太婆衣履端正，_____。（过新年）

　④　傍晚日光西射，建筑物构成的阴带_____。（遮阳伞）

2. 纳凉的芸芸众生时而西瓜，**时而**凉粉，**时而**大麦茶绿豆汤和莲子百合红枣汤。

> **时而**……**时而**……

　①　人们都坐卧在弄堂里，_____，_____。（聊天、享受美食）

　②　大龙和伊人为了感受上海人的生活，出行时_____，_____。（公交车、地铁）

　③　老太婆_____，_____拿出来。（轻摇羽扇、银耳羹）

　④　老头子_____，_____。（小菜、白兰地）

文化理解练习 Cultural Reading Comprehension

小词库 Word Bank

- 附近　fùjìn　nearby, vicinity
- 高楼大厦
  gāolóu dàshà　skyscraper

📋 **读一读，选一选** Read and Choose

1. 我是大龙，这次和伊人一起来上海游玩。昨天我们去了上海的外滩。外滩附近有很多高楼大厦。今天我们打算去看看老上海的弄堂，听说上海的弄堂和北京的胡同不太一样，条数巨万，纵的、横的、斜的、曲的都有。

❓他们今天要去看什么？

　A 斜街　　B 弄堂

　C 胡同　　D 四合院

文化小词库 Cultural Word Bank

- 外滩　　　Wài Tān
  Waitan, the Bund in Shanghai

2. 我是伊人。今天我们学习了课文《弄堂风光》，里面提到老上海的有钱人盛夏时都喜欢去一个地方避暑，今年暑假我也打算去那里。

❓ 今年暑假伊人打算去哪里？

A 长城　　B 黄山　　C 拙政园　　D 庐山

课堂文化交际 Cultural Communication

 小组活动 Group Activity

选词填空，完成对话。再两人一组练习对话。

▌对话一 Dialogue 1

> 胡同　巨万　纵的　斜的　迷魂阵

 有朋，你听说过上海的弄堂吗？

 上海的弄堂条数 _____，_____、横的、_____、曲的都有，你想问我哪条弄堂呢？

 按你的说法，上海的弄堂如同一个 _____ 啊！

 是啊！上海的弄堂和北京的 _____ 差别很大，在弄堂里很容易迷路。

 是吗？那倒是挺有趣的。我真想去感受感受！

对话二 Dialogue 2

藤椅　小板凳　时而　羽扇　笔挺　啜

今天咱们看的老上海电影真有意思。夏天大家都跑到弄堂里来纳凉了。

是啊！_____、竹榻、帆布床、_____，都摆到弄堂里来了，整个弄堂都难于通行。

大家一边纳凉，一边吃好吃的，_____ 西瓜，_____ 凉粉，_____ 大麦茶绿豆汤、莲子百合红枣汤，好热闹啊！

那位衣履端正的老奶奶正轻摇 _____；那位穿着 _____ 的老爷爷正 _____ 他的法国三星白兰地，好不惬意啊！

课后文化实践 Cultural Practice

👤 **个人活动** Individual Activity

上海知名的弄堂有哪些？这些弄堂是因什么而知名的？请你试着在网上查一查，下节课给大家讲一讲！

上海的弄堂	1.	2.	3.	4.
因何知名				

弄堂 *Longtang* (Lane)

　　弄堂即小巷，是上海、江苏、浙江地区特有的民居形式，它是由连排的老房子所构成的，并与石库门建筑有着密切的关系。弄堂曾经是普通上海人最常见的生活空间，它也是近代上海城市最重要的建筑特色，创造了形形色色、风情独具的弄堂文化，是近代上海城市文化的重要组成部分。弄堂可分为广式里弄、新式石库门里弄、新式里弄、花园式里弄等形式。其中，上海的典型弄堂有：王家楼、左家宅、亨昌里、范园、春光坊、姚村、薛家库、涌泉坊。

Longtang are lanes characteristic of Shanghai, Zhejiang and Jiangsu. Closely related to Shikumen (Stone-ringed Door)-style architecture, *longtang* form a unique dwelling mode consisted of old terraced houses. In modern Shanghai, *longtang* were once the most commonplace living space for ordinary urban dwellers and the most significant local architectural style. The diverse, exotic *longtang* culture created thereon also became an integral cultural component of modern urban Shanghai. The various types of *longtang* include Cantonese-style *lilong* (namely, longtang), new Shikumen-style *lilong*, new-style *lilong*, and garden-style *lilong*. The most typical *longtang* in Shanghai are Wangjia Lou (the Wang-Family Building), Zuojia Zhai (the Zuo-Family Manor), Hengchang Li (Hengchang Neighbourhood), Fan Yuan (the Fan Garden), Chunguang Fang (Spring-Light Lane), Yao Cun (Yao Village), Xuejia She (the Xue-Family Village), and Yongquan Fang (Bubbling Spring Lane).

外滩 The Bund

　　外滩位于上海市中心黄浦区的黄浦江畔，长约 1.5 千米。外滩是旧上海时期的金融中心，外滩西侧矗立着数十幢风格各异的高楼，素有"外滩万国建筑博览群"的美誉，它们表征着上海城市的历史，见证了上海昔日的辉煌。与外滩隔江相对的浦东陆家嘴则坐落着东方明珠、金茂大厦、上海中心大厦、上海环球金融中心等新上海的标志性建筑，这些建筑是中国改革开放成就的象征和上海现代化建设的缩影。

The Bund, about 1.5 kilometers long, is located on the banks of the Huangpu River in the Huangpu District of Shanghai. The Bund was a financial center in the old Shanghai era. On the west side of the Bund stands dozens of high-rise buildings of various styles known as "the Exotic Building Cluster in the Bund of Shanghai." They represent the history of Shanghai and witnessed the glory of old Shanghai. Across the river and opposite the Bund is Lujiazui Financial Zone in Pudong New Area, home to Shanghai Oriental Pearl Radio and TV Tower, Shanghai Jinmao Tower, Shanghai Tower, Shanghai World Financial Center and other landmark buildings of new Shanghai. These buildings are the symbol of China's reform and opening up, and the epitome of Shanghai's modernisation.

03

第 **3** 课
Lesson 3

Xī'ān zhè zuò chéng
西安这座城

热身活动 Warm Up

1. 请你给大家介绍一个有名的上海弄堂。
2. 你去过西安吗？你觉得西安是一座什么样的城市？

课 文 Text

时至今日，气派不倒的，风范依存的，在全世界的范围内最具古城魅力的城市，西安是其中之一。它的城墙赫然完整，独身站定在护城河上的吊板桥上，仰观那城楼、角楼，再怯懦的人也要豪情长啸了。大街小巷方正对称，排列有序的四合院砖雕门楼下已经黝黑如铁的花石门墩，让你可以立即坠入了古昔里高头大马拉着木制的大车喤喤喤开过来的境界里去。如果有机会收集一下全城的数千个街巷名称，你会突然感到

历史并不遥远，以至眼前飞过一只不卫生的苍蝇，也忍不住怀疑这苍蝇的身上有着汉时的模样或有唐时的标记。现代的艺术日夜在上演着，但爬满青苔的如古钱一样的城墙根下，总是有人在观赏着中国最古老的属于这个地方的秦腔，或者皮影木偶。

（摘编自《西安这座城》，有删改）

生 词 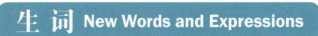 New Words and Expressions

1.	气派	qìpài	dignified air
2.	倒	dǎo	fall, collapse
3.	风范依存	fēngfàn yīcún	of past glamour
4.	范围	fànwéi	range
5.	具	jù	possess, have
6.	古城	gǔchéng	ancient city
7.	魅力	mèilì	charm
8.	赫然	hèrán	awesomely
9.	完整	wánzhěng	complete
10.	仰观	yǎngguān	look up
11.	怯懦	qiènuò	timid and overcautious
12.	豪情长啸	háoqíng chángxiào	let out a long cry of lofty ambitions
13.	大街小巷	dàjiē xiǎoxiàng	big streets and small alleys; all the streets in the area
14.	排列有序	páiliè yǒuxù	orderly arranged
15.	黝黑如铁	yǒuhēi rútiě	dark as iron
16.	立即	lìjí	immediately
17.	坠入	zhuìrù	fall into
18.	古昔	gǔxī	antiquity

19.	高头大马	gāotóu dàmǎ	tall horse
20.	喤喤喤	huánghuánghuáng	an onomatopoeic word describing the sound of heavy vehicles passing by, vroom
21.	境界	jìngjiè	realm
22.	收集	shōují	collect
23.	突然	tūrán	suddenly
24.	遥远	yáoyuǎn	remote
25.	以至	yǐzhì	so much so (that...)
26.	眼前	yǎnqián	in front of one's eyes
27.	苍蝇	cāngying	fly (insect)
28.	忍不住	rěnbuzhù	cannot help but
29.	怀疑	huáiyí	doubt
30.	模样	múyàng	appearance, look
31.	标记	biāojì	mark, sign
32.	艺术	yìshù	art
33.	上演	shàngyǎn	enact
34.	青苔	qīngtái	green moss
35.	城墙根下	chéngqiáng gēn xià	by the foot of the city wall

文化词语
Cultural Words

1. 护城河　　hùchéng hé　　moat
2. 吊板桥　　diàobǎn qiáo　　hanging bridge
3. 城楼　　chénglóu　　gate tower
4. 角楼　　jiǎolóu　　turret
5. 四合院　　sìhéyuàn　　Siheyuan, Chinese courtyard
6. 砖雕门楼　　zhuān diāo ménlóu　　gate house with carved bricks
7. 花石门墩　　huā shí méndūn　　porphyry gate pier
8. 秦腔　　qínqiāng　　Qinqiang Opera, a folk Chinese opera originated in Shaanxi, China
9. 皮影木偶　　píyǐng mùǒu　　shadow puppet

课文理解练习 Text Comprehension

 根据课文选一选 Choose the Right Answers Based on the Text

1. 文中认为全世界最具古城魅力的是哪座城市?

北京

西安

上海

苏州

2. 以下哪项不属于西安的特色?

秦腔

皮影

兵马俑　　熊猫

💬 **根据提示说一说** Complete the Sentences Based on the Given Clues

1. ……**以至**眼前飞过一只不卫生的苍蝇，也忍不住怀疑这苍蝇的身上有着汉时的模样或有唐时的标记。 ……**以至（于）**……

   ❶ 因为住惯了这样布局齐整的地方，_____。（外省，迷路转向）

   ❷ 四合院砖雕门楼下的花石门墩因年代久远显得非常老旧，_____。（黝黑如铁）

   ❸ 西安的城墙赫然完整、宏伟壮观，_____。（怯懦的人，豪情长啸）

   ❹ 我很喜欢西安的古城文化，_____。（秦腔）

2. ……以至眼前飞过一只不卫生的苍蝇，也**忍不住**怀疑这苍蝇的身上有着汉时的模样或有唐时的标记。 ……**忍不住**……

   ❶ 如果有机会去西安，你会_____。（兵马俑）

   ❷ 仰观西安的城楼、角楼，你会_____。（豪情长啸）

   ❸ 看到黝黑如铁的花石门墩，你会_____。（古昔里的高头大马）

   ❹ 上海的夏天很热，傍晚的时候，人们_____。（弄堂）

文化理解练习 Cultural Reading Comprehension

 读一读，选一选 Read and Choose

　　我是大龙，今天上课的时候，我们学习了中国作家贾平凹的散文《西安这座城》，使我对西安产生了兴趣。我了解到西安曾经叫长安，中国曾有十三个封建王朝在这里建都。在古代中国的汉唐时期，西安十分繁华，是国家的政治、经济、军事、文化中心。

1. 西安曾经叫作什么？

[A] 洛阳　　[B] 长安　　[C] 大都　　[D] 咸阳

2. 中国有多少个王朝曾在西安建都？

[A] 十一　　[B] 十二　　[C] 十三　　[D] 十四

文化小词库 Cultural Word Bank

- 长安　Cháng'ān　Chang'an, the old name of Xi'an
- 王朝　wángcháo　dynasty
- 建都　jiàndū　establish the capital

课堂文化交际 Cultural Communication

 小组活动 Group Activity

选词填空，完成对话。再两人一组练习对话。

对话一 Dialogue 1

赫然完整　高头大马　城楼　角楼　豪情长啸　方正对称　排列有序　境界

 伊人，你觉得中国哪座城市最有古城魅力？

我最喜欢西安，因为那里的城墙_____。

 是啊！独身站在护城河的吊板桥上，仰观那_____和_____，再怯懦的人也要_____了。

西安的大街小巷_____，四合院也是_____的。

走在西安的大街小巷，让人可以立即坠入古昔里 _____
拉着木制的大车喤喤喤开过来的 _____ 里去。

对话二 Dialogue 2

肉夹馍　臊子面　秦腔　皮影木偶　兵马俑

有朋，西安有哪些名胜古迹呢？

西安最有名的是秦始皇陵、_____ 和华清池。

这些我都看过了呢！

那我建议你听听 _____，看看 _____，也都很有特色。

谢谢！我最喜欢这些曲艺节目了！对了，西安有什么特色小吃吗？

哈哈！你又问对人了！西安的 _____ 和 _____ 最好吃了！

文化小词库 Cultural Word Bank

- 秦始皇陵　Qínshǐhuáng Líng　The Mausoleum of the First Qin Emperor
- 华清池　Huáqīng Chí　Huaqing Pool
- 肉夹馍　ròujiāmó　Ruojiamo, pork belly buns, a street food in Xi'an
- 臊子面　sàozi miàn　Saozi noodles, mince noodles, a street food in Xi'an

课后文化实践 Cultural Practice

个人活动 Individual Activity

选择一处你去过的或者你感兴趣的西安的名胜古迹，下节课给大家介绍一下吧！

西安的名胜古迹	推荐理由

西安 Xi'an

　　西安，古称长安，现为陕西省省会。西安地处渭河平原中部，北濒渭河，南依秦岭，历史上先后有十三个王朝在此建都，是中国著名的古都之一。西安是中华文明重要发祥地之一，也是古代丝绸之路的起点。西安是中国第一批国家历史文化名城之一。西安目前有多处遗产被列入《世界遗产名录》，如秦始皇陵及兵马俑坑等。此外，西安还有大雁塔、小雁塔、钟鼓楼、碑林等著名的旅游景点。

Xi'an, known in ancient times as Chang'an, is today's provincial capital of Shaanxi Province. Situated in the Weihe Plain, Xi'an neighbours River Wei to the north and the Qin Mountains to the south. Throughout its history, 13 dynasties have made Xi'an their capitals, making it one of the famous ancient capitals of China. Xi'an is a significant cradle for the Chinese civilization, and also served as the starting point of the Silk Road. Xi'an is also among the very first national historic cities of China. Xi'an boasts several UNESCO World Heritage Sites, such as the Mausoleum of the First Qin Emperor and the Terracotta Warriors. Tourist attractions also abound in Xi'an, such as the Big Wild Goose Pagoda, the Little Wild Goose Pagoda, the Bell and Drum Towers, and Xi'an Beilin Museum, etc.

秦腔 Qinqiang Opera

秦腔是中国西北地区的传统戏剧，流行于陕西、甘肃等地，是中国最古老的戏剧之一。2006 年秦腔入选第一批中国国家级非物质文化遗产名录。因为古时陕西、甘肃一带属秦国，所以称之为"秦腔"。早期秦腔演出时，常用枣木梆子敲击伴奏，故又名"梆子腔"。秦腔的表演技艺朴实、粗犷、豪放，富有夸张性，生活气息浓厚，技巧丰富，因其表演体系成熟完整，流传于中国各地，对其他剧种产生了不同程度的影响。秦腔脸谱是舞台美术的有机组成部分，绘制风格古典独特，与京剧脸谱、川剧脸谱一起形成中国曲艺特有的脸谱系统。

Qinqiang Opera is a traditional opera in Northwest China. As one of the most ancient operas of China, Qinqiang is popular in Shaanxi Province and Gansu Province. In 2006, it became one of the first Chinese National Intangible Cultural Heritages. Back in ancient times, the area of today's Shaanxi Province and Gansu Province was under the rule of the Qin State, hence the opera was named as "Qinqiang (Qin Tune)". In the early stages of Qinqiang, jujube wood clappers were often used to accompany Qinqiang performance, therefore the opera is also called "Bangziqiang (Clapper Tune)". Qinqiang performance is characterised by a simple, bold, exquisite yet exaggerated style that showcases a wealth of vitality and skills. Owing to its mature and complete performance system, Qinqiang has spread across the country and impacted on other operatic forms to various degrees. An organic component of the ancient art of Qinqiang is its face painting. Unique and classical in its style, Qinqiang ranks among the great face painting systems of Chinese operas along with Beijing and Chuan Operas.

单元自评
Self-Assessment

本单元我们学习了有关中国"城市文化"的中文表达和文化知识。请你用下面的表格检查一下自己的学习成果吧！如果 5 个中国结是满分，你会给自己几个呢？In this unit, we have learned expressions and cultural knowledge about *Culture in Cities*. Please make use of the table below to evaluate your learning. If five Chinese knots mean full completion, how many will you give yourself?

第 1 课		🎴	🎴🎴	🎴🎴🎴	🎴🎴🎴🎴	🎴🎴🎴🎴🎴
🏮 我会使用下列句型。	·一……，总是……					
	·以……为……					
🏮 我知道下列中国文化知识。	·胡同					
	·烟袋斜街					
🏮 我能为朋友介绍北京的胡同。						
第 2 课		🎴	🎴🎴	🎴🎴🎴	🎴🎴🎴🎴	🎴🎴🎴🎴🎴
🏮 我会使用下列句型。	·……如/如同……（一般）					
	·时而……时而……					
🏮 我知道下列中国文化知识。	·弄堂					
	·外滩					
🏮 我能为朋友介绍上海的弄堂。						
第 3 课		🎴	🎴🎴	🎴🎴🎴	🎴🎴🎴🎴	🎴🎴🎴🎴🎴
🏮 我会使用下列句型。	·……以至（于）……					
	·……忍不住……					
🏮 我知道下列中国文化知识。	·西安					
	·秦腔					
🏮 我能为朋友介绍西安的名胜古迹。						

扩展 Further Extension

🏮 关于中国"城市文化"，我还了解以下内容：

1. _____

2. _____

第二单元
UNIT ❷

建筑文化
Culture in Architecture

04

Gùgōng : qiānpiān yílǜ
故宫：千篇一律

yǔ qiānbiàn wànhuà
与千变万化

课 文 Text

热身活动 Warm Up

1. 请给大家介绍一处西安的名胜古迹。
2. 你去过北京的故宫吗？你对故宫印象最深的是什么？为什么？

在艺术创作中，往往有一个重复和变化的问题。只有重复而无变化，作品就必然单调枯燥；只有变化而无重复，就容易陷于散漫零乱。古今中外的无数建筑，除去极少数例外，几乎都以重复作为取得艺术效果的重要手段之一。

历史中杰出的例子是北京的明清故宫。从天安门到端门、午门是一间间重复着的"千篇一律"的朝房。再进去，"前三殿"与"后三宫"是大同小异的重复，就像乐曲中的主题和"变奏"；而东西两侧的廊、庑、楼、门，又是比较低微的，以重复为主但亦有相当变化的"伴奏"。然而整个故宫，它的每一个组群，每一个殿、阁、廊、门却全部都是按照统一规格、统一形式建造的，连彩画、雕饰也尽如此，都是无尽的重复。我们完全可以说它们"千篇一律"。

但是，谁能不感到，从天安门一步步走进去，就如同置身于一幅大"手卷"里漫步；在时间持续的同时，空间也连续着"流动"。那些殿堂、楼门、廊庑虽然制作方法千篇一律，然而每走几步，前瞻后顾、左睇右盼，那整个景色的轮廓、光影，却都在不断地改变着，一个接着一个新的画面出现在周围，千变万化。空间与时间，重复与变化的辩证统一在北京故宫中达到了最高的成就。

（摘编自《千篇一律与千变万化》，有删改）

生 词 New Words and Expressions

1.	千篇一律	qiānpiān yílù	stereotyped		11.	零乱	língluàn	messy
2.	创作	chuàngzuò	creation		12.	古今中外	gǔjīn zhōngwài	in the past and the present, at home and abroad
3.	往往	wǎngwǎng	often		13.	无数	wúshù	countless
4.	重复	chóngfù	repetition		14.	除去	chúqù	except
5.	作品	zuòpǐn	work		15.	极少数	jí shǎoshù	few
6.	必然	bìrán	necessity		16.	例外	lìwài	except for
7.	单调	dāndiào	monotonous		17.	取得	qǔdé	achieve
8.	枯燥	kūzào	dull		18.	效果	xiàoguǒ	effect
9.	容易	róngyì	easy		19.	手段	shǒuduàn	method
10.	散漫	sǎnmàn	undisciplined					

20.	杰出	jiéchū	distinguished
21.	大同小异	dàtóng xiǎoyì	virtually the same
22.	乐曲	yuèqǔ	music
23.	主题	zhǔtí	theme
24.	变奏	biànzòu	variation
25.	伴奏	bànzòu	accompaniment
26.	组群	zǔqún	group
27.	按照	ànzhào	according to
28.	彩画	cǎihuà	colour painting
29.	雕饰	diāoshì	carving
30.	置身（于）	zhìshēn (yú)	place oneself (in)

31.	手卷	shǒujuàn	hand scroll
32.	漫步	mànbù	stroll
33.	前瞻后顾	qiánzhān hòugù	look forward and backward, look around
34.	左睇右盼	zuǒdì yòupàn	look to the left and right, look around
35.	轮廓	lúnkuò	outline
36.	成就	chéngjiù	achievement
37.	光影	guāngyǐng	light and shadow
38.	周围	zhōuwéi	surrounding
39.	辩证统一	biànzhèng tǒngyī	dialectical unity

文化词语

Cultural Words

1.	端门	Duān Mén	Duan Gate
2.	午门	Wǔ Mén	the Meridian Gate
3.	朝房	cháofáng	reception room for officials (in former times)
4.	前三殿	qián sān diàn	the First Three Halls of the Palace Museum, namely *Taihe Dian* (Hall of Supreme Harmony), *Zhonghe Dian* (Hall of Central Harmony), and *Baohe Dian* (Hall of Preserving Harmony)
5.	廊	láng	veranda
6.	庑	wǔ	side room
7.	殿	diàn	hall
8.	阁	gé	pavilion, cabinet

课文理解练习 Text Comprehension

 根据课文选一选　Choose the Right Answers Based on the Text

1. 故宫的每个组群是按照什么形式建造的？

A 流动的形式　　　　　B 变化的形式

C 不同的形式　　　　　D 统一的形式

2. 本文认为空间与时间、重复与变化的辩证统一在哪里中达到了最高的成就？

北京故宫

苏州拙政园

敦煌莫高窟

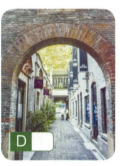
上海弄堂

💬 **根据提示说一说**　Complete the Sentences Based on the Given Clues

1. 除去极少数例外，几乎都以重复作为取得艺术效果的重要手段之一。

> 以……作为……

❶ 建筑的重复与变化，可以 ＿＿＿＿＿＿。（北京明清故宫、杰出的例子）

❷ 中国的人造卫星是 ＿＿＿＿＿＿。（嫦娥、名字）

❸ 故宫的每一个殿、阁、廊、门都 ＿＿＿＿＿＿。（重复、取得艺术效果的重要手段）

❹ 中国历史上有十三个朝代 ＿＿＿＿＿＿。（西安、都城）

2. **在**时间持续**的同时**，空间也连续着"流动"。 在……的同时……

① 故宫的殿堂、楼门、廊庑 ＿＿＿＿＿＿＿。（千篇一律、千变万化）

② 今天我游览故宫，＿＿＿＿＿＿＿。（参观展览、买些网红的故宫文创产品）

③ 大龙想去西安旅行，因为 ＿＿＿＿＿＿＿。（参观兵马俑、听秦腔）

④ 北京是一个旅游胜地，＿＿＿＿＿＿＿。（古代名胜古迹、现代建筑）

小词库 Word Bank

- 胜地　shèngdì　**resort**

文化理解练习 Cultural Reading Comprehension

读一读，选一选 Read and Choose

1. 我是大龙，今天和伊人去了坐落在北京市中心的城中之城——紫禁城，现在人们叫它"故宫"，也叫"故宫博物院"。我们参观了太和殿、保和殿、乾清宫和坤宁宫。

❓ 下面哪个图片不是故宫里的景点？

| 太和殿 | 乾清宫 | 坤宁宫 | 颐和园 |

文化小词库 Cultural Word Bank

- 太和殿　Tàihé Diàn　　*Taihe Dian* (Hall of Supreme Harmony)
- 保和殿　Bǎohé Diàn　　*Baohe Dian* (Hall of Preserving Harmony)
- 乾清宫　Qiánqīng Gōng　*Qianqing Gong* (Palace of Heavenly Purity)
- 坤宁宫　Kūnníng Gōng　*Kunning Gong* (Palace of Earthly Tranquility)

2. 故宫是明清两代的皇宫，也是世界上现存最大、最完整的木结构宫殿建筑群。它是中国古代建筑艺术中的精品。故宫宫殿沿着一条南北向中轴线排列，前三殿、后三殿（即后三宫）、御花园都位于这条中轴线上，南北取直，左右对称。这条中轴线不仅贯穿在故宫内，而且南达永定门，北到鼓楼、钟楼，贯穿了整个老北京城，气魄宏伟，规划严整，极为壮观。

❓ 故宫是哪两个朝代的皇宫？

A 唐、宋 B 明、清

C 隋、唐 D 元、明

小词库 Word Bank

- 精品 　　 jīngpǐn 　　 fine works (of art)
- 中轴线 　 zhōngzhóuxiàn 　 the Central Axis
- 气魄宏伟 　 qìpò hóngwěi 　 magnificent
- 规划严整 　 guīhuà yánzhěng 　 well-organised

文化小词库 Cultural Word Bank

- 御花园 　 yùhuāyuán 　 the Royal Garden
- 永定门 　 Yǒngdìng Mén 　 Yongding Gate (Forever Peace Gate)

课堂文化交际 Cultural Communication

 小组活动 Group Activity

选词填空，完成对话。再两人一组练习对话。

对话一 Dialogue 1

前三殿　后三宫　辩证统一　变化　重复

 我今天又去了故宫，这是我第三次去故宫了。

_____、_____、御花园，你都转了吗？

我转了太和殿、中和殿、保和殿 _____ 。还有乾清宫、交泰殿、坤宁宫 _____ 。这次我没转御花园。

故宫里的大部分建筑都是大同小异的重复。你为什么要去这么多次？

有 _____ ，也有 _____ 。我觉得 _____ 与 _____ 的 _____ 在北京故宫中达到了最高的成就。

文化小词库 Cultural Word Bank

- 中和殿　Zhōnghé Diàn　**Zhonghe Dian (Hall of Central Harmony)**
- 交泰殿　Jiāotài Diàn　**Jiaotai Dian (Hall of Union and Peace)**

▌对话二 Dialogue 2

轮廓　光影　杰作　殿　阁　廊　门　手卷　千变万化　千篇一律

有朋，你能给我讲讲故宫建筑的特点吗？

大龙，你可真是勤学善问！故宫的每一个 _____ 、_____ 、_____ 、_____ 都是按照统一规格、统一形式建造的，是无尽的重复。

彩画和雕饰也如此吗？

是的，完全可以说是 _____ 。

那为什么中国人都认为故宫是中国建筑史上的 _____ 呢?

 人在故宫里,每走几步,前瞻后顾、左睇右盼,整个景色的 _____、_____ 就会不断地改变,故宫又是 _____ 的。

 听起来真有意思!有朋,你可真是个学识渊博的大才子啊!

 哈哈!谢谢大龙!中国著名建筑学家梁思成才是真正的才子,他曾经说从天安门一步步走进故宫,就如同置身于一幅大"_____"里漫步。

 听你讲完,我还想再去故宫感受一次!

小词库 Word Bank

- 勤学善问　qínxué shànwèn
  diligent and inquisitive
- 学识渊博　xuéshí yuānbó
  erudite

课后文化实践 Cultural Practice

 个人活动 Individual Activity

有人喜欢故宫的建筑,有人喜欢故宫的藏品,还有人喜欢故宫猫和故宫的文创产品,你对故宫里的什么最感兴趣?下节课给大家说说吧!

我对故宫最感兴趣的事物

太和殿 *Taihe Dian* (Hall of Supreme Harmony)

太和殿，俗称"金銮殿"，是中国现存最大的木结构大殿之一。它位于北京故宫南北中轴线的显要位置，是故宫内体量最大、等级最高的建筑物。明清两朝 24 位皇帝都在太和殿举行盛大典礼，如皇帝即位、皇帝大婚、册立皇后、命将出征，此外每年万寿（皇帝生日）、元旦、冬至三大节，皇帝在此接受文武官员的朝贺，并向王公大臣赐宴。太和殿于明永乐十八年（1420 年）建成，原称奉天殿。明嘉靖四十一年（1562 年）改称皇极殿，清顺治二年（1645 年）改今名。太和殿自建成后屡遭焚毁，又多次重建，今殿为清康熙三十四年（1695 年）重建后的形制。

Taihe Dian (Hall of Supreme Harmony), commonly referred to as *Jinluan Dian* (Hall of Golden Chimes), is one of the largest of all existing wood structure halls in China. It is located at a prominent position on the north-south axis of the Palace Museum in Beijing, and *Taihe Dian* is the largest hall and the highest-ranked building in the Museum. Twenty-four emperors of the Ming and Qing Dynasties had held grand ceremonies here, such as enthronement, wedding, empress crowning, army deployment, along with the three major holidays — Wanshou (Emperor's Birthday), New Year, and the Winter Solstice. It was also here where the emperors received courtesy from civil and military officials and held feasts for imperial princes and court ministers. First built in the 18th year of Emperor Yongle's reign (1420) as *Fengtian Dian* (Hall of Offering to Heaven), it was renamed as *Huangji Dian* (Hall of Imperial Supremacy) in the 41st year of Emperor Jiajing's reign (1562), before the Qing Emperor Shunzhi changed it to the present name in the second year of his reign (1645). Since its construction, *Taihe Dian* has gone through many fires and reconstructions, and what we see today is the result of the reconstruction undertaken in the 34th year of Kangxi's reign (1695).

乾清宫 *Qianqing Gong* (Palace of Heavenly Purity)

乾清宫是内廷正殿，是所谓"后三宫"（乾清宫、交泰殿、坤宁宫）中的第一座宫殿。乾清宫面阔 9 间，进深 5 间，高 20 余米，重檐庑殿顶，殿的正中有宝座，东西两侧有暖阁。宝座上方悬着由清朝顺治皇帝御笔亲书的"正大光明"匾。乾清宫是明清 16 位皇帝的寝宫。在乾清宫前露台两侧有两座石台，石台上各设一座鎏（liú）金铜亭，称作"江山社稷金殿"，俗称"金亭子"。金亭子圆形攒尖式，上层檐上安有铸造古雅的宝顶，象征江山社稷掌握在皇帝手中。

Qianqing Gong (Palace of Heavenly Purity) is the main palace in the inner living area of the Forbidden City, and also the first of the three rear residential palaces, the other two being *Jiaotai Dian* (Hall of Union and Peace) and *Kunning Gong* (Palace of Earthly Tranquility). Standing over 20 metres tall, *Qianqing Gong* is 9 rooms in width and 5 rooms in depth, with a double-eave Wudianding roof. In the middle of the palace is the throne and on the east and west side are warm pavillions. Above the throne hangs a plaque board inscribed with "Fair and Square" by Qing Emperor Shunzhi. *Qianqing Gong* was the living residence of 14 Ming emperors and 2 Qing emperors. The front terrace of *Qianqing Gong* is flanked with two stone platforms, on each of which is placed a gilded copper pavilion called "Golden Pavilion of the Rivers, Mountains, Earth and Grain" or colloquially *Jin Tingzi* (Golden Pavilion). On the upper round pyramidal roof of each pavilion is a genteel dome, which symbolises the emperor's control of everything under heaven.

05

第5课
Lesson 5

Lǎo Běijīng sìhéyuàn
老北京四合院

热身活动 Warm Up

1. 说一说你对故宫的什么最感兴趣。
2. 你知道老北京人住的房子是什么样的吗？请简单描述一下。

课文 Text

老北京四合院之好，在于它有房子、有院子、有大门、有房门。关上大门，自成一统；走出房门，顶天立地；四顾环绕，中间舒展，廊栏曲折，有露有藏。如果条件好，几个四合院连在一起，那除去"合"之外，又多了一个"深"

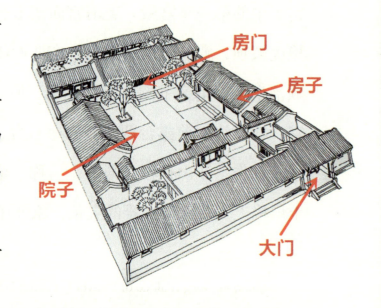

房门

房子

院子

大门

字。"庭院深深深几许""一场愁梦酒醒时，斜阳却照深深院"……这样中国式的诗境，其感人深处，是和古老的四合院建筑分不开的。

四合院好在其"合"，贵在其"敞"。"合"便于保存自我的天地；"敞"则更容易观赏广阔的空间，视野更大，无坐井观天之弊。这样的居住条件，似乎也影响到居住者的素养气质：一是不干扰别人，自然也不愿别人干扰；二是很敞快、较达观、不拘谨、较坦然，但也缺少竞争性，自然也不斤斤计较；三是对自然界很敏感，对春夏秋冬的岁时变化有深厚情致。

（摘编自《老北京四合院》，有删改）

生 词 New Words and Expressions
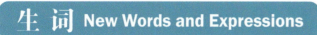

1.	在于	zàiyú	lie in
2.	自成一统	zìchéng yìtǒng	unique in its own system
3.	四顾环绕	sìgù huánrào	connected on the four sides
4.	舒展	shūzhǎn	extend
5.	曲折	qūzhé	meandering
6.	合	hé	closeness
7.	贵	guì	highly valued
8.	敞	chǎng	spacious, open
9.	便于	biànyú	easy to
10.	保存	bǎocún	preserve
11.	广阔	guǎngkuò	vast
12.	视野	shìyě	vision
13.	弊	bì	disadvantage
14.	居住	jūzhù	live
15.	条件	tiáojiàn	condition
16.	似乎	sìhū	seemingly
17.	居住者	jūzhùzhě	resident
18.	素养	sùyǎng	personal quality
19.	气质	qìzhì	temperament
20.	干扰	gānrǎo	disturb
21.	敞快	chǎngkuài	cheerful
22.	达观	dáguān	optimistic
23.	拘谨	jūjǐn	over-cautious
24.	坦然	tǎnrán	honest
25.	缺少	quēshǎo	lack
26.	竞争性	jìngzhēngxìng	competitiveness
27.	斤斤计较	jīnjīn jìjiào	calculating and unwilling to make any sacrifice
28.	自然界	zìránjiè	nature
29.	敏感	mǐngǎn	sensitive
30.	岁时	suìshí	seasons and time of the year
31.	深厚	shēnhòu	deep
32.	情致	qíngzhì	emotion

文化词语
Cultural Words

1. 顶天立地	dǐngtiān lìdì	stand upright on one's own two legs between heaven and earth
2. 有藏有露	yǒucáng yǒulòu	covering some while showing others
3. 庭院深深深几许	tíngyuàn shēnshēn shēn jǐ xǔ	Deep, deep is the courtyard.
4. 一场愁梦酒醒时，斜阳却照深深院	yì chǎng chóu mèng jiǔ xǐng shí, xiéyáng què zhào shēnshēn yuàn	When I woke up from a sad dream, the setting sun was shining on the deep courtyard.
5. 诗境	shījìng	the realm of poetry
6. 坐井观天	zuòjǐng guāntiān	view the sky from the bottom of the well

课文理解练习 Text Comprehension

 根据课文选一选 Choose the Right Answers Based on the Text

1. 四合院之好，在于它有什么？

A 房子、院子、大门、房门

B 房子、院子、大门、窗户

C 房子、院子、房门、阳台

D 房子、院子、房门、房檐

2. 住在北京四合院里的人会形成什么样的素养气质？（多选）

A 不干扰别人

B 很敞快、较达观

C 对自然界很敏感

D 较拘谨、不坦然

💬 **根据提示说一说** Complete the Sentences Based on the Given Clues

1. 那**除去**"合"**之外**，又多了一个"深"字。 　**除去/除了……之外……**

　　① 夏季外出避暑 ＿＿＿＿＿＿＿，还可以去黄山。（庐山）

　　② 说起有代表性的老北京建筑，＿＿＿＿＿＿＿，就是老北京四合院了。
　　（皇家宫殿）

　　③ 清明节的习俗 ＿＿＿＿＿＿＿，还有踏青郊游。（扫墓祭祖）

　　④ 四合院居住者的性格，＿＿＿＿＿＿＿，还不拘谨。（敞快）

2. 这样中国式的诗境，其感人深处，**是和**古老的四合院建筑**分不开的**。 　**……是和……分不开的**

　　① 故宫文创产品能够成为网红商品，＿＿＿＿＿＿。（新颖的文化创意）

　　② 西安能够成为热门旅游目的地，＿＿＿＿＿＿。（它悠久的历史文化）

　　③ "一带一路"倡议的发起 ＿＿＿＿＿＿。（古代丝绸之路）

　　④ 四合院居住者的素养气质 ＿＿＿＿＿＿。（居住条件）

文化理解练习 Cultural Reading Comprehension

读一读，选一选 Read and Choose

1. 我是大龙。我发现在北京城大大小小的胡同中，坐落着一些由东、南、西、北四面房屋围合起来的院落式住宅，后来有朋告诉我这是老北京人的民居，叫"四合院"。

北京胡同中由四面房屋围合起来的院落式住宅叫什么？

A 弄堂　　　　B 四合院　　　　C 斜街　　　　D 别墅

2. 我叫王富贵，是北京人。北京人不习惯到别的城市居住，我们这个大家庭一直住在四合院里。四合院是我们北京人世代居住的主要建筑形式，历史悠久，一般是正方形或者长方形的院落。在寸土寸金的北京，我们一家人能住在一个院子里，过着悠闲的生活，享受大家庭的快乐，我感到很幸福。

? 四合院是哪里人居住的主要建筑形式？

A 老北京人　　B 老四川人　　C 老西安人　　D 老上海人

小词库 Word Bank

- 历史悠久　lìshǐ yōujiǔ　with a long history
- 寸土寸金　cùntǔ cùnjīn　(of land) extremely expensive
- 悠闲　yōuxián　leisurely

课堂文化交际 Cultural Communication

 小组活动　Group Activity

选词填空，完成对话。再两人一组练习对话。

对话一 Dialogue 1

合　房子　院子　环绕　舒展　曲折　诗境　露　藏

李晶，你刚带我逛了老北京的胡同，接下来咱们去哪里呢？

老北京的四合院很有特点，我带你看看四合院吧！咱们已经到了，这就是四合院！

这里真不错！有 _____、有 _____、有大门、有房门。

是啊！四顾 _____，中间 _____，廊栏 _____，有 _____ 有 _____。

北京所有的四合院都和这个院子一样吗？

有比这个更大的，几个四合院连在一起，那除去"_____"之外，又多了一个"深"字。正如诗句"庭院深深深几许"写的那样。

看来中国式的 _____ 和古老的四合院建筑也是分不开的呀！

对话二 Dialogue 2

敞　合　坐井观天　拘谨　素养气质

李晶，老北京人为什么喜欢住四合院呢？

北京四合院好在其"_____"，贵在其"_____"。"_____"便于保存自我的天地；"_____"则更容易观赏广阔的空间，视野更大，无 _____ 之弊。

这样的居住条件对居住者的 _____ 有什么影响吗？

居住者的性格会比较敞快、达观、不 _____。

课后文化实践 Cultural Practice

你喜欢老北京的四合院吗？请想想四合院有什么优点和缺点，下次课和大家一起讨论一下。

老北京的四合院

优点	缺点

北京四合院 Beijing *Siheyuan* (Courtyards)

　　四合院又称"四合房"，是一种中国传统合院式住宅。所谓"四合"，"四"指东、西、南、北四个方向，"合"即四面房屋围在一起，形成一个"口"字形的结构。经过数百年的历史，北京四合院从平面布局到内部结构和装修都形成了特有的京味风格。北京四合院一般有内外两院，内院是住宅的中心，围绕院子，四面布置有北房（正房）、南房（倒座房）和东、西厢房，四周再以高墙连接围合。四合院的院落宽绰疏朗，四面房屋各自独立，彼此之间有走廊连接，人们住在里面起居方便，活动自如。

Beijing *siheyuan* (literally "quadrangular courtyard"), also known as *sihefang* (quadrangular house), is a traditional Chinese building compound. "*Si* (four)" refers to the four directions of east, west, north and south; "*he* (closed)" means that the houses on the four sides of the courtyard are combined into one "口"-shaped compound, hence the term *siheyuan*. Through hundreds of years of evolution, Beijing *siheyuan* has developed a unique Beijing style in terms of layout, interior, and decoration. A standard *siheyuan* in Beijing mostly has south-facing main gates, with rooms on four sides — Beifang (north house, also known as Zhengfang, main house), Nanfang (south house, also known as Daozuofang, reverse-facing house) and Xiangfang (side house) on the east and west sides. A high wall runs around the houses, forming a spacious courtyard with only one main gate. The houses on four sides are connected by corridors and each house enjoys relative independence. *Siheyuan* provides convenience and spacious living conditions.

坐井观天 *Zuo Jing Guan Tian* (Sit in a Well and Look at the Sky)

成语"坐井观天"的意思是坐在井底看天，比喻和讽刺眼界狭窄、学识肤浅，常用来指那些盲目自大、不接受新事物、不识大局的人。这则成语出自唐代诗人韩愈的《原道》："坐井而观天，曰天小者，非天小也。"意思是说，坐在井里观察天空，就会觉得天很小很小；其实不然，不是天太小，而是由于看天的人站得低、眼光太窄，所以看到的天才显得很小。坐井观天的近义词有：井底之蛙、鼠目寸光、管中窥豹、一叶障目、管窥蠡测、盲人摸象。

The idiom 坐井观天, which means to "sit in a well and look at the sky", is an ironic reference to narrow-minded, ignorant yet conceited people who do not accept new things or fail to see the important issues. The origin of this idiom is from the essay titled *Yuan Dao* (*The Original Way*) by poet Han Yu of the Tang Dynasty: "Someone who sits in a well and looks at the sky might say the sky is small, which is not the case". If one observes the sky from the bottom of a well, the sky would appear to be very small, but such illusion does not stem from the size of the sky, but rather the low position and narrow vision of the observer. Similar idioms include: 井底之蛙 (the frog at the bottom of a well), 鼠目寸光 (a mouse is short-sighted), 管中窥豹 (peek at the leopard through a tube), 一叶障目 (cannot see the forest for the leaf is in front of one's eyes), 管窥蠡测 (peek at the sky through a tube and measure the sea with a calabash), and 盲人摸象 (blind people can only get to know an elephant by touching and thus may not have a holistic picture).

Láng · tíng · qiáo
廊·亭·桥

课 文 Text

廊

　　"别梦依依到谢家，小廊回合曲阑斜。"一千多年前的唐诗，点出了廊在庭院中的妙用。中国古代建筑的单体与单体之间，必依靠廊来做联系，才能成为一个整体。廊在园林中是游览线，又起着分隔空间、组合景物的作用。廊引人随，水石其间，移步换影，幅幅成图。像驰名中外的北京颐和园的长廊，漫步其间，得以饱览昆明湖的湖光景色。而苏州拙政园的水廊，轻盈婉约，人行其上，宛如凌波漫步。扬州西园前的香影廊，未至其境，名已醉人。

亭

　　人们在游览中，每见一亭，总想小憩片刻，借以缓解疲劳与观赏四周的景色，即"亭者，停也"。北京的景山五亭，地理位置高，吸引人们来此饱览首都景色。苏州拙政园的扇面亭，亭名"与谁同坐轩"，小亭临流，静观自得。而网师园的"月到风来亭"又正点出此亭观景之妙。至于亭的形式，真是变化多端，可分为方、圆、多边等多种。它在园林建筑中展示了最美丽的一页。

桥

　　桥是架在水上的行道。中国古代人民把桥和生活、感情、艺术结合起来，富于诗情画意。北京颐和园十七孔长桥卧波陆水之间，为颐和园增添了几许光彩。江南园林之桥，以雅洁精巧取胜。而水平线条的石桥，则贴水而过，观赏游鳞莲藻，益得情趣。美丽的中国园林桥梁，形式丰富多样，有梁式桥、拱桥、浮桥、廊桥、亭桥等，在世界建筑艺术上放出一种独特光彩。

（摘编自《廊·亭·桥》，有删改）

生 词 New Words and Expressions

1.	点出	diǎn chū	point out
2.	单体	dāntǐ	single
3.	依靠	yīkào	rely on
4.	成为	chéngwéi	become
5.	整体	zhěngtǐ	unity
6.	游览线	yóulǎn xiàn	sight-seeing route
7.	分隔	fēngé	separate
8.	组合	zǔhé	integrate
9.	景物	jǐngwù	scenery
10.	作用	zuòyòng	effect
11.	廊引人随	láng yǐn rén suí	the veranda leads people to walk along
12.	移步幻影	yí bù huàn yǐng	(of scenery) change with each step
13.	饱览	bǎolǎn	feast one's eyes on something
14.	轻盈	qīngyíng	light
15.	婉约	wǎnyuē	graceful
16.	宛如	wǎnrú	as if
17.	凌波漫步	língbō mànbù	walk over ripples
18.	小憩	xiǎoqì	take a short rest
19.	片刻	piànkè	a moment

20.	缓解	huǎnjiě	alleviate
21.	疲劳	píláo	fatigue
22.	四周	sìzhōu	all around, on all sides
23.	吸引	xīyǐn	attract
24.	首都	shǒudū	capital
25.	形式	xíngshì	form
26.	变化多端	biànhuà duōduān	change in various ways
27.	展示	zhǎnshì	display
28.	架	jià	prop up
29.	结合	jiéhé	combine
30.	诗情画意	shīqíng huàyì	poetic beauty
31.	卧波	wòbō	(figurative use of bridges) lie on the waves
32.	增添	zēngtiān	add to
33.	以……取胜	yǐ...qǔ shèng	win out by ...
34.	雅洁精巧	yǎjié jīngqiǎo	elegant and exquisite
35.	贴水而过	tiē shuǐ ér guò	sweep past water
36.	游鳞	yóu lín	swimming fish
37.	莲蕖	liánqú	lotus
38.	独特	dútè	unique

文化词语
Cultural Words

1. 颐和园　　　Yíhé Yuán　　　the Summer Palace
2. 昆明湖　　　Kūnmíng Hú　　　Kunming Lake
3. 香影廊　　　Xiāngyǐng Láng　　　Xiangying Veranda
4. 景山五亭　　Jǐngshān wǔ tíng　　five pavilions of Jingshan
5. 月到风来亭　Yuèdào Fēnglái Tíng　Yuedao Fenglai Pavilion
6. 十七孔长桥　Shíqīkǒng Chángqiáo　Seventeen-Arch Bridge

课文理解练习 Text Comprehension

 根据课文选一选 Choose the Right Answers Based on the Text

1. 中国古代建筑的单体与单体之间，必依靠什么来做联系，才能成为一个整体？

廊　　　　　　亭　　　　　　桥　　　　　　梁

2. 哪里有一座名为"与谁同坐轩"的扇面亭？

北京景山　　　苏州拙政园　　　北京颐和园　　　苏州网师园

💬 **根据提示说一说** Complete the Sentences Based on the Given Clues

1. 廊在园林中是游览线，又**起着**分隔空间、组合景物**的作用**。

起着……的作用

  1 廊在中国古代建筑中 _____。（单体）

  2 "亭者，停也"，亭在游览中 _____。（小憩）

  3 水平线条的石桥，贴水而过，_____。（观赏）

  4 港珠澳大桥 _____。（香港、珠海、澳门）

2. 江南园林之桥，**以**雅洁精巧**取胜**。

以……取胜

  1 北京故宫 _____。（气势宏伟）

  2 苏州拙政园的水廊，_____，人行其上，宛如凌波漫步。
    （轻盈婉约）

  3 北京的景山五亭 _____。（地理位置）

  4 扬州西园前的香影廊，_____，未至其境，名已醉人。（名字）

文化理解练习 Cultural Reading Comprehension

读一读，想一想 Read and Think

文化小词库 Cultural Word Bank

1. "别梦依依到谢家，小廊回合曲阑斜。"
   是唐代诗人张泌的诗歌《寄人》的头两句。

   ❓ 张泌写出了廊的何种建筑特点？

   A 笔直   B 歪斜   C 曲折回环   D 圆形

- 张泌　　Zhāng Bì
  Zhang Bi, poet of the Tang Dynasty
- 《寄人》"Jì rén"
  To Someone in Dream,
  a poem by Zhang Bi

2. 我是大龙，周末我想去一个地理位置高的地方，饱览首都北京的风景。

❓ 大龙周末会去下面哪个地方？

A 景山公园　　B 颐和园　　C 长城　　D 天坛

课堂文化交际 Cultural Communication

 小组活动 Group Activity

选词填空，完成对话。再两人一组练习对话。

对话一 Dialogue 1

| 昆明湖　分隔　组合　长廊　十七孔长桥 |

 李晶，我发现中国的许多园林都建有长廊，廊有什么作用呢？

 在园林中起着 _____ 空间、_____ 景物的作用。

 是这样啊！我最喜欢北京颐和园的 _____，漫步其间，可以饱览 _____ 的湖光景色。

 我最喜欢颐和园的 _____，它卧波陆水之间，为颐和园增添了几许光彩。

对话二 Dialogue 2

饱览　景山五亭　拙政园　变化多端

有朋，我想 _____ 北京的景色，去哪个地方比较好呢？

那要找个地理位置高的地方才行啊！北京人常去 _____ 饱览北京的景色。

你说的这些亭子漂亮吗？

在中国，亭的形式 _____，有方、圆、多边等多种，亭在园林建筑中展示了最美丽的一页。

我去过苏州 _____ 的扇面亭，我特别喜欢那里，至今难忘。

课后文化实践 Cultural Practice

👤 个人活动 Individual Activity

请总结一下课文里一共提到了多少处廊、亭、桥，选其中的一处查找其详细资料和图片，下次课介绍给大家。

课文里一共有：廊 _____ 处、亭 _____ 处、桥 _____ 处

我选择的景观	特色介绍	图片

拙政园 The Humble Administrator's Garden

拙政园位于江苏省苏州市，始建于明正德初年（16 世纪初），是江南古典园林的代表。拙政园与北京颐和园、承德避暑山庄、苏州留园并称为中国四大名园。拙政园全园以水为中心，山水萦绕，厅榭精美，花木繁茂，具有浓郁的江南水乡特色。花园分为东、中、西三部分，各具特色，其中，中花园是全园精华所在。园南为住宅区，体现典型江南地区传统民居多进的格局。著名景点有见山楼、听雨轩、小飞虹等。1997 年拙政园被列入联合国教科文组织的《世界遗产名录》，2007 年被评为首批中国国家 5A 级旅游景区。

Built in the first year of the Ming Emperor Zhengde's reign (the beginning of the 16th century) in today's Suzhou, Jiangsu Province, the Humble Administrator's Garden is a representative Suzhou classic garden. It is one of the four most famous Chinese gardens along with the Summer Palace in Beijing, the Mountain Resort in Chengde, and Lingering Garden in Suzhou. The Humble Administrator's Garden is centred on water with winding hills and streams, exquisite halls, water pavilions, and exuberant vegetation, and it gives rise to a rich characteristic of Jiangnan water towns. The Humble Administrator's Garden consists of East, Central and Western sections, each with its own unique features. The Central section is the true essence of the Garden. The southern part of the Garden contains residential houses with multiple courtyards, which is typical of traditional residences in the Jiangnan area. Famous attractions in the Humble Administrator's Garden include Jianshan Lou (Mountain-in-View Tower), Tingyu Xuan (Listen-to-the-Rain Pavilion) and Xiaofeihong (Small Flying Rainbow Bridge). Listed as a UNESCO World Heritage Site in 1997, the Humble Administrator's Garden was nominated as one of the first National 5A Tourist Scenic Areas in 2007.

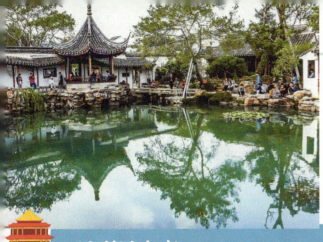

月到风来亭　Yuedao Fenglai Pavilion

　　月到风来亭位于江苏省苏州市网师园的彩霞池西，亭名取意宋代邵雍诗句"月到天心处，风来水面时"。此亭踞西岸水涯而建，三面环水。亭东二柱上，挂有清代何绍基的题字"园林到日酒初熟，庭户开时月正圆"。月到风来亭是临风赏月的好地方，特别是金秋时节，天高气爽，此时的风爽于别日，月明于平时，天上明月高悬，池中皓月相映，金桂盛放，香气满园。

　　Yuedao Fenglai Pavilion is located to the west of Caixia Chi (Rosy Cloud Pond) in the Master-of-Nets Garden in Suzhou City, Jiangsu Province. The name of the Pavilion originated from a poem by Song Dynasty poet Shao Yong, "The moon travels to the heart of heaven; the wind lands on the surface of water". The Pavilion sits on the west bank of the river and is enclosed by water on three sides. Hanged on a couple of pillars in the east of the Pavilion are the inscription by Qing Dynasty poet He Shaoji, "Wine was mature when we arrived at the garden; we opened the windows to a full moon." One can savour the most stylish fun of the Pavilion when one admires the moon in the wind and cool air in golden autumn. During this time of year, the wind is cooler and the moon is fuller than usual. The bright moon high above is accompanied by its reflection in the pond, the sweet fragrance of osmanthus blossoms wafts through the garden.

单元自评
Self-Assessment

本单元我们学习了有关中国"建筑文化"的中文表达和文化知识。请你用下面的表格检查一下自己的学习成果吧！如果 5 个中国结是满分，你会给自己几个呢？In this unit, we have learned expressions and cultural knowledge about *Culture in Architecture*. Please make use of the table below to evaluate your learning. If five Chinese knots mean full completion, how many will you give yourself?

第 4 课		🏮	🏮🏮	🏮🏮🏮	🏮🏮🏮🏮	🏮🏮🏮🏮🏮
🏮 我会使用下列句型。	·以……作为……					
	·在……的同时……					
🏮 我知道下列中国文化知识。	·太和殿					
	·乾清宫					
🏮 我能为朋友介绍故宫。						
第 5 课		🏮	🏮🏮	🏮🏮🏮	🏮🏮🏮🏮	🏮🏮🏮🏮🏮
🏮 我会使用下列句型。	·除去……之外……					
	·……是和……分不开的					
🏮 我知道下列中国文化知识。	·北京四合院					
	·坐井观天					
🏮 我能说出北京四合院的特点。						
第 6 课		🏮	🏮🏮	🏮🏮🏮	🏮🏮🏮🏮	🏮🏮🏮🏮🏮
🏮 我会使用下列句型。	·起着……的作用					
	·以……取胜					
🏮 我知道下列中国文化知识。	·拙政园					
	·月到风来亭					
🏮 我能为朋友介绍中国亭、廊、桥的特点。						
扩展 Further Extension						

🏮 关于中国"建筑文化"，我还了解以下内容

1. _____

2. _____

第三单元
UNIT ③

服饰文化
Culture in Costume

第7课
Lesson 7

Bǎinián zhōngshānzhuāng
百年中山装

课文 Text

中山装因孙中山提倡而得名，被视为中国典型的现代服装。1911年辛亥革命后，中国提倡"剪辫易服"，人们设计制作了一款新式礼服——中山装。后来经过反复修改，中山装最终形成"封闭式小翻领、袖口边三个扣、四袋五扣"的上衣样式，并开始在中国流行。

渐渐地中山装的很多细节被赋予了文化含义：中山装的四个口袋代表礼、义、廉、耻，前面五颗扣子代表孙中山倡导的区别于西方三权分立的五分立权，即行政、立法、司法、考试、监察。袖子上的三颗扣子代表三民主义，即民族、民权、民生。后背是由一整块面料制作而成，代表了国家的统一。上衣口袋带盖、带尖，叫"倒笔架"，代表对文化和知识分子的尊重。

新中国成立后，中国人都非常喜欢穿中山装。现在，中山装已经成为中国男装一款标志性的服装。

生 词 New Words and Expressions

1.	新式礼服	xīnshì lǐfú	new-style suit
2.	反复	fǎnfù	repetitive
3.	修改	xiūgǎi	modify
4.	形成	xíngchéng	form
5.	封闭式	fēngbìshì	closed
6.	小翻领	xiǎofānlǐng	narrow turn-down collar
7.	袖口	xiùkǒu	cuff
8.	上衣	shàngyī	top
9.	样式	yàngshì	design
10.	口袋	kǒudai	pocket
11.	扣子	kòuzi	button
12.	代表	dàibiǎo	represent
13.	区别	qūbié	distinguish
14.	行政	xíngzhèng	administration
15.	立法	lìfǎ	legislation
16.	司法	sīfǎ	jurisdiction
17.	监察	jiānchá	supervision
18.	民权	mínquán	Principle of Democracy, civil rights
19.	民生	mínshēng	Principle of the People's Livelihood
20.	后背	hòubèi	back
21.	面料	miànliào	fabric
22.	男装	nánzhuāng	men's clothes
23.	款	kuǎn	style
24.	标志性	biāozhìxìng	iconic

文化词语
Cultural Words

1. 辛亥革命	Xīnhài Gémìng	Revolution of 1911
2. 剪辫易服	jiǎn biàn yì fú	the cutting of the "queue" (men's braid) and the change of clothing
3. 礼义廉耻	lǐ yì lián chǐ	rite, righteousness, honesty and shame
4. 三权分立	Sānquán Fēnlì	Separation of (the Three) Powers
5. 三民主义	Sānmín Zhǔyì	"Three People's Principles" (Nationalism, Democracy and People's Livelihood, as put forward by Dr. Sun Yat-Sen)
6. 倒笔架	dào bǐjià	inverted pen-rack

课文理解练习 Text Comprehension

 根据课文选一选 Choose the Right Answers Based on the Text

1. 中山装的四个口袋代表什么？

 A 勤劳勇敢

 B 自强不息

 C 礼义廉耻

 D 忠孝节义

2. 下列哪个不是中山装的特征？

 A 前面有五粒扣子

 B 袖子上有两粒扣子

 C 后背是一整块的面料

 D 口袋带盖带尖

💬 **根据提示说一说**　Complete the Sentences Based on the Given Clues

1. 孙中山倡导的区别于西方三权分立的五分立权，即行政、立法、司法、考试、监察。

> **……，即……**

❶ 故宫有三大殿，＿＿＿＿＿＿＿、＿＿＿＿＿＿＿、＿＿＿＿＿。
（太和殿、中和殿、保和殿。）

❷ 中国有两个特别行政区，＿＿＿＿＿＿＿。（香港、澳门）

❸ 孙中山倡导三民主义，＿＿＿＿＿＿＿。（民族、民权、民生）

❹ 中国提出建设"一带一路"倡议，＿＿＿＿＿＿＿。（"丝绸之路经济带"和"21世纪海上丝绸之路"）

2. 中山装是不破缝的，后背是由一整块面料制作而成。

> **……是由……制作而成**

❶ 饺子＿＿＿＿＿＿＿。（饺子皮、馅）

❷ 这件唐装＿＿＿＿＿＿＿。（丝绸）

❸ 宫保鸡丁＿＿＿＿＿＿＿。（鸡丁、花生、干辣椒）

❹ 莲子百合红枣汤＿＿＿＿＿＿＿。（莲子、百合、红枣）

文化理解练习　Cultural Reading Comprehension

📋 **读一读，选一选**　Read and Choose

1. 我是大龙，今天我学习了关于中山装的知识。我了解到中山装前面的五粒扣子代表孙中山倡导的行政、立法、司法、考试、监察五分立权。袖子上的三粒扣子代表民族、民权、民生三民主义。我发现中山装里大有学问啊！

?中山装袖子上的三粒扣子代表什么？

A 民族、民权、立法 　　B 民权、民生、考试

C 民族、民权、行政 　　D 民族、民权、民生

2. 我是伊人，今天我学习了关于中山装的知识。我了解到中山装的后背由一整块面料制作而成，代表了国家的统一。上衣口袋带盖、带尖，叫"倒笔架"，代表对文化和知识分子的尊重。

?中山装的上衣口袋带盖、带尖代表着什么？

A 国家的统一

B 治国严谨

C 代表对文化和知识分子的尊重

D 三民主义

课堂文化交际 Cultural Communication

 小组活动 Group Activity

选词填空，完成对话。再两人一组练习对话。

| 对话一 Dialogue 1

礼义廉耻　倒笔架　一百多　三民主义　对文化和知识分子的尊重

 大龙，中山装有 _____ 年的历史了，你知道中山装有哪些特点吗？

我知道中山装的四个口袋代表 _____，袖子上的三粒扣子代表
_____。

你知道中山装的上衣口袋带盖、带尖叫什么吗？

口袋带盖带尖叫 _____，代表 _____。

大龙，你太棒了！中山装不仅穿起来帅气，而且它还具有丰富的文化内涵。

对话二 Dialogue 2

标志性　倡导　孙中山　中山装　现代服装

李晶，这种衣服为什么叫中山装呢？

中山装是因 _____ 而得名，被视为中国典型的 _____。

哦！我看很多照片里，中国男性都穿着中山装呢！

在中国，很多人都喜欢穿 _____。现在，中山装成为中国男装一款 _____ 的服装。

课后文化实践 Cultural Practice

👤 个人活动　Individual Activity

除了中山装以外，中国还有很多其他具有代表性的服饰，请你找一找相关资料，下次课给大家讲一讲。

中山装 The Chinese Tunic Suit (Zhongshan Suit)

中山装造型大方、严谨，因孙中山先生喜爱穿着并倡导而得名。辛亥革命后中山装在中国流行，被视为中国典型的现代服装。中山装的推广与流行，促成了中国传统袍式服装向西方短式服装的转型，改变了中国人"交领右衽、上衣下裳"的服饰传统，也改变了中国人对服装的审美习惯。中山装对于引导人们形成共同的政治、思想、文化与情感认同等都起到了积极作用。

The Chinese tunic suit (Zhongshan Suit) is elegant and rigorous in style. And it is named after Dr. Sun Yat-Sen's love and support. After the Revolution of 1911, Chinese tunic suits became popular in China and was then regarded as typical modern clothing. The spread and popularity of tunic suits contributed to the transformation of traditional Chinese gowns to the Western short style garments. This changed Chinese peoples' dressing habit of "crossover collar and right lapel, upper and lower garment." The taste of Chinese people in clothing habits has also changed. The tunic suit has played a positive role in guiding people to form a common ground in political, ideological, cultural and emotional identity.

礼义廉耻 The Four Social Bonds (Rite, Righteousness, Honesty and Shame)

　　礼义廉耻出自《管子·牧民》，是管仲协助齐桓公推行政令时所依循的准则。礼是指礼制，义是指义气、道义、正义感，廉是指廉洁方正，耻是指有知耻之心。孔子说过："知耻近乎勇"，意思是知道错误就去改过，为当所为，是勇敢的表现。《新五代史·杂传》曰："礼义廉耻，国之四维。四维不张，国乃灭亡。"礼、义是治人之大法，廉、耻是立人之大节。不廉则无所不取，不耻则无所不为，人若如此，则祸败乱亡，无所不至；大臣若无所不取，无所不为，则天下必乱，国家必亡。因此，"礼义廉耻"指的是社会的道德标准和行为规范。

From *Guan Zi·Herdsman,* the Four Social Bonds (rite, righteousness, honesty and shame) was the criterion Guan Zhong followed when assisting Duke Huan of Qi in pushing the administrative order. Li (礼) refers to rite. Yi (义) refers to righteousness, morality, and a sense of justice. Lian (廉) refers to honesty and clean. And Chi (耻) refers to a sense of shame. Confucius said, "To know shame is close to be brave" which means to correct the mistakes when you know them and to do what you should do is a sign of bravery. *The New History of the Five Dynasties · Miscellaneous Biography* said: "Rite, righteousness, honesty and shame are the four social bonds of a country. If the four social bonds are not there, the country will perish." Rite and righteousness are great methods in governing people, while honesty and shame are great methods in building people. If you are not honest, you will take everything. And if you are shameless, you will do everything. If people are like this, then fortune will fail and perish, and thus misfortune will occur. If the ministers take everything and do everything, then the world will be in chaos and the country will perish. Therefore, "rite, righteousness, honesty and shame" refer to the social moral standards and codes of conduct.

08

第8课
Lesson 8

Sòng Qìnglíng hé qípáo
宋庆龄和旗袍

课文 Text

宋霭龄、宋庆龄、宋美龄是中国历史上著名的"宋氏三姐妹"，她们是 20 世纪初中国影响力很大的女性人物。宋氏三姐妹都曾在美国留学。在着装上，她们三人都偏爱旗袍。

宋庆龄是孙中山先生的夫人，1925 年孙中山先生去世后，她的服饰一直以深色调的旗袍为主，素雅是宋庆龄旗袍的一个显著特点。现在的旗袍两侧开衩很高，而当时宋庆龄穿的旗袍开衩都很低，最高的也仅及于膝盖。

抗战时期，宋庆龄曾经送给一位美国友人一件中式旗袍。这位美国友人正是穿着这件旗袍，为中国筹集了很重要的一笔援助资金。

从三十多岁到七十多岁，无论是接待外宾，还是到国外出访，身着旗袍的宋庆龄，显得高雅脱俗，她把旗袍穿成了中国的"国服"。

生 词 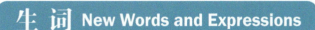 New Words and Expressions

1.	著名	zhùmíng	famous
2.	影响力	yǐngxiǎnglì	influence
3.	着装	zhuózhuāng	clothing
4.	偏爱	piān'ài	prefer
5.	深色调	shēn sèdiào	dark tones
6.	素雅	sùyǎ	simple but elegant
7.	显著	xiǎnzhù	distinctive
8.	特点	tèdiǎn	feature
9.	两侧	liǎngcè	both sides
10.	开衩	kāichà	split, opening
11.	及于	jí yú	reach to
12.	膝盖	xīgài	knee
13.	正是	zhèngshì	exactly
14.	筹集	chóují	raise (funding)
15.	资金	zījīn	funding
16.	接待	jiēdài	receive
17.	外宾	wàibīn	foreign guest
18.	出访	chūfǎng	visit a foreign country
19.	高雅脱俗	gāoyǎ tuōsú	graceful and distinguished

文化词语

Cultural Words

1. 宋霭龄　Sòng Ǎilíng　Soong Eling
2. 宋庆龄　Sòng Qìnglíng　Soong Ching-Ling
3. 宋美龄　Sòng Měilíng　Soong May-Ling
4. 宋氏三姐妹　Sòngshì sān jiěmèi　Three Sisters of the Soong Family
5. 旗袍　qípáo　cheongsam
6. 国服　guófú　national dress

课文理解练习 Text Comprehension

 根据课文选一选 Choose the Right Answers Based on the Text

1. 孙中山先生的夫人是（　　）。

A 宋霭龄

B 宋庆龄

C 宋美龄

2. 宋霭龄、宋庆龄、宋美龄在着装上都很喜欢（　　）。

马褂

旗袍

西装

中山装

💬 **根据提示说一说** Complete the Sentences Based on the Given Clues

1. 她的服饰一直以深色调的旗袍为主。 ……以……为主

❶ 他的衣服 ＿＿＿＿＿＿＿＿。（黑色）

❷ 北京的街道 ＿＿＿＿＿＿＿＿。（正南正北、正东正西）

❸ 老北京人的民居 ＿＿＿＿＿＿＿＿。（四合院）

❹ 中国人的主食 ＿＿＿＿＿＿＿＿。（米饭和面条）

2. 素雅是宋庆龄的旗袍的一个显著特点。 ……是……的一个显著特点

❶ 开衩很低 ＿＿＿＿＿＿＿＿。（宋庆龄的旗袍）

❷ 深色调 ＿＿＿＿＿＿＿＿。（宋庆龄的旗袍）

❸ 带尖、带盖 ＿＿＿＿＿＿＿＿。（中山装口袋）

❹ 后背不破缝 ＿＿＿＿＿＿＿＿。（中山装）

文化理解练习 Cultural Reading Comprehension

 读一读，选一选 Read and Choose

1. 我是伊人。今天我了解到宋庆龄很喜欢穿旗袍。我也是个旗袍爱好者，我的旗袍两侧开衩很高，颜色鲜艳。我的旗袍和宋庆龄的不一样，她喜欢穿素雅的深色调旗袍，她的旗袍开衩都很低，最高的也仅及于膝盖。我看了很多张宋庆龄的照片，穿着旗袍的她从容端庄、高雅脱俗。

❓ 下列哪一项属于宋庆龄的旗袍的特点？

Ａ 两侧开衩很高　Ｂ 素雅的浅色调　Ｃ 两侧开衩很低　Ｄ 颜色很鲜艳

2. 我是大龙。今天我了解到在 20 世纪初，很多中国女性都穿旗袍，那时候的旗袍宽大平直，下摆比较大。后来，旗袍吸收了西方服饰的特色，变得更加合身。现在，在中国举办的奥运会、亚运会等国际大型活动经常选择旗袍作为礼仪服装。

❓20 世纪初的旗袍有什么特点？

A 宽大平直　　　B 下摆比较小

C 吸收了西方特色　　D 更加合身

小词库 Word Bank

- 下摆　　xiàbǎi
  lower hem
- 合身　　hé shēn
  well-fitting
- 奥运会　Àoyùnhuì
  the Olympic Games
- 亚运会　Yàyùnhuì
  the Asian Games

文化小词库 Cultural Word Bank

- 礼仪服装　　　lǐyí fúzhuāng
  etiquette clothing

课堂文化交际 Cultural Communication

 小组活动 Group Activity

选词填空，完成对话。再两人一组练习对话。

对话一 Dialogue 1

宋氏三姐妹　深色调　素雅　宋庆龄　开衩

伊人，你听说过中国著名的"宋氏三姐妹"吗？

这个问题难不倒我。在美国的时候，我就听过 _____ 的故事。我知道她们都很美丽，而且她们都很喜欢穿旗袍。

对！_____ 是孙中山先生的夫人，她经常穿 _____ 的旗袍。

我还听说宋庆龄的旗袍以 _____ 为主，旗袍 _____ 都很低，最高的也仅及于膝盖。

伊人，没想到你是旗袍"专家"啊！

小词库 Word Bank

- 专家　zhuānjiā　expert

▍对话二 Dialogue 2

资金　穿旗袍　中式旗袍　国服

有朋，今天我听老师讲宋庆龄不仅自己喜欢 _____，而且曾经送给一位美国友人一件 _____。

是啊，这位美国友人正是穿着这件旗袍，为中国筹集了很重要的一笔援助 _____。

身着旗袍的宋庆龄给人的感觉真是高雅脱俗啊！

宋庆龄把旗袍穿成了中国的"_____"。

课后文化实践 Cultural Practice

👤 **个人活动**　Individual Activity

旗袍在不同的时期有不同的流行样式，请你找一找相关的图片，下次课给大家介绍一下。

时期　　　　　样式　　　　　特点

旗袍 Cheongsam

旗袍原为清朝满族妇女所穿用的一种服装，两边不开衩，袖长八寸至一尺，衣服的边缘绣有彩绿。20 世纪 20 年代，旗袍被改良为直领，右斜襟开口，紧腰身，衣长至膝下，两边开衩，紧袖口，颇受当时的女性青睐。旗袍曾被指定作为中国女性外交人员礼服。在中国举办的大型国际活动中多采用旗袍作为礼仪服装。旗袍作为中国女性代表性服饰，不仅能展现出东方女性的独特魅力和气质，还带动了丝绸、服装等行业领域的发展。

Cheongsam was originally a kind of clothing worn by Manchu women in the Qing Dynasty. The dress did not have slits on both sides and the sleeves were eight to twelve *cun* (equals to 1.31 inches) long. The edges of the dress are also embroidered with the colour green. In the 1920s, the cheongsam was modified as follows: a straight collar, right oblique flap opening, a tight waist, dress length reaching below the knee, slit on both sides and tight cuffs. It was quite popular with women at that time. Cheongsam was once known as the formal dress of Chinese female diplomats. And it was often used as ceremonial clothing in various international events held in China. As the representative clothing of Chinese women, cheongsam not only presents the unique charm and temperament of oriental women, but also advances the development of silk, clothing and other industries.

宋氏三姐妹 Three Sisters of Soong Family

宋霭龄、宋庆龄、宋美龄被称为"宋氏三姐妹"，她们出生于19世纪末的上海。宋庆龄与孙中山结婚，他们共同捍卫共和制。孙中山逝世后，宋庆龄继续为中国人民的解放事业做贡献。1949年中华人民共和国成立，宋庆龄当选为中华人民共和国中央人民政府副主席，在承担大量国务活动的同时，她把大量精力投入到了妇女与儿童的文化、教育、卫生与福利事业中。

Soong Eling, Soong Ching-Ling, and Soong May-Ling were known as the "Three Sisters of the Soong Family". They were born in the late 19th century in Shanghai. The middle sister Soong Ching-Ling married Sun Yat-Sen and both were committed defenders of republicanism. After Sun Yat-Sen died from illness, Soong Ching-Ling did not stop her efforts for the liberation of the Chinese people. At the foundation of the People's Republic of China in 1949, Soong Ching-Ling was elected Vice Chairman of the Central People's Government of People's Republic of China. While managing a great amount of state affairs, she also devoted much energy to enhancing women's and children's literacy, education, sanitation and welfare.

09

第9课
Lesson 9

Wèishénme chuān tángzhuāng?

为什么穿唐装？

课文 Text

热身活动 Warm Up

1. 请给大家讲讲不同时期的旗袍的特点。
2. 你听说过唐装吗？你知道唐装有哪些特点吗？

　　我是电影演员成龙。在美国拍《炮弹飞车》的时候，好莱坞还没有人认识我。我在电影里饰演一个日本人，在片场就被国外演员当成日本人，我解释了也没什么用。那段时间，我出席很多活动都穿西装。大家问我是哪里人，"Where are you from?（你从哪里来？）" "Hong Kong.（香港。）"那个时候他们都不知道香港在哪里。在很多地方，亚洲人在他们眼里长得都差不多，再都穿西装，根本分不出来。那时候我就想，不行，以后我要你们一看衣服就知道我是中国人，所以我就开始穿唐装。久而久之，人家一看就知道，哦，你是中国人。

　　后来真的在全世界都有名了之后，唐装就变成了我的一个标志，到哪里都不会跟别人撞衣服，永远都是很特别的。你们看很多女明星害怕撞衫，但我很少会跟别人撞衫。

（摘编自《为什么穿唐装》，有删改）

生 词 New Words and Expressions

1.	拍	pāi	shoot (a film)
2.	饰演	shìyǎn	play the role of ...
3.	片场	piànchǎng	set
4.	演员	yǎnyuán	actor, actress
5.	当成	dāngchéng	treat ... as ...
6.	解释	jiěshì	explain
7.	出席	chūxí	attend

8.	久而久之	jiǔ'ér jiǔzhī	as time goes by
9.	人家	rénjia	other people
10.	标志	biāoshì	symbol
11.	永远	yǒngyuǎn	forever
12.	好莱坞	Hǎoláiwū	Hollywood
13.	撞衫	zhuàng shān	accidentally wear the same clothes

文化词语
Cultural Words

1.	唐装	tángzhuāng	Tang suit
2.	成龙	Chéng Lóng	Jackie Chen, Chinese *Kung Fu* star

课文理解练习 Text Comprehension

根据课文选一选
Choose the Right Answers Based on the Text

1. 成龙在美国拍摄《炮弹飞车》的时候，国外演员认为他是（　　）人。

 美国　　 英国　　 中国　　 日本

2. 成龙是（　　）人。

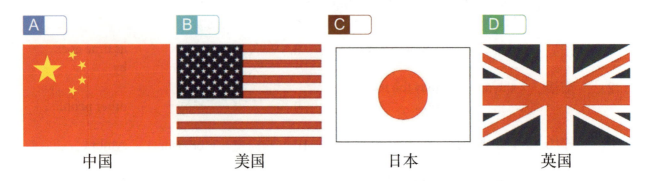

A　　　　　　B　　　　　　C　　　　　　D

中国　　　　　美国　　　　　日本　　　　　英国

💬 **根据提示说一说** Complete the Sentences Based on the Given Clues

1. 我在电影里饰演一个日本人，在片场就被国外演员当成日本人。

　　　　　　　　　　　　　　　　　　　被……当成……

① 共享单车 ＿＿＿＿＿＿＿＿。（外国人、中国的"新四大发明"）

② "亭者，停也"，亭 ＿＿＿＿＿＿＿＿。（中国人、停下来休息的地方）

③ 大熊猫 ＿＿＿＿＿＿＿＿。（中国人、国宝）

④ 孔子 ＿＿＿＿＿＿＿＿。（中国人、万世之师）

2. 唐装就变成了我的一个标志。　　　……变成/是……的标志

① 西湖 ＿＿＿＿＿＿＿＿。（杭州）

② 拙政园 ＿＿＿＿＿＿＿＿。（苏州）

③ 十七孔桥 ＿＿＿＿＿＿＿＿。（颐和园）

④ 扇面亭的亭名是"与谁同坐轩"，它 ＿＿＿＿＿＿＿＿。（拙政园）

文化理解练习 Cultural Reading Comprehension

 读一读，选一选 Read and Choose

1. 我是有朋。成龙是我最喜欢的功夫明星。我觉得成龙不仅电影演得棒，而且还非常爱国。成龙最初出席活动的时候，很多人不知道他是哪国人。为了让更多外国人知道自己是中国人，成龙开始穿唐装。因此，唐装也就成了成龙的一个标志。

❓ 成龙为什么开始穿唐装？

A 穿唐装是拍电影的需要。　B 穿唐装是出席活动的需要。

C 功夫明星需要穿唐装。　D 为了体现自己是中国人。

2. 我是大龙。我非常喜欢中国功夫，我最崇拜的明星是成龙。成龙很喜欢穿唐装，这让我也对唐装产生了兴趣，我去查了关于唐装的资料。我了解到，唐装主要使用真丝等面料，款式结构有四大特点：一是立领；二是连袖，即袖子和衣服整体没有接缝；三是对襟，也可以是斜襟；四是盘扣。

❓ 以下哪些属于唐装的特点？（多选）

A 立领。

B 连袖，袖子和衣服整体有接缝。

C 对襟，也可以是斜襟。

D 盘扣。

小词库 Word Bank

- 崇拜　chóngbài　worship
- 真丝　zhēnsī　silk
- 款式　kuǎnshì　style
- 接缝　jiēfèng　seam
- 扣子　kòuzi　button

文化小词库 Cultural Word Bank

- 立领　lǐlǐng　stand collar
- 连袖　liánxiù　raglan sleeve
- 对襟　duìjīn　Chinese style clothing with buttons down the front
- 斜襟　xiéjīn　Chinese style clothing with buttons down the side
- 盘扣　pánkòu　Chinese knot button, frog button

课堂文化交际 Cultural Communication

 小组活动 Group Activity

选词填空，完成对话。再两人一组练习对话。

▌对话一 Dialogue 1

唐装　日本人　《炮弹飞车》　香港　西装　亚洲人　中国人

 大龙，你看过成龙演的电影吗？

 当然看过！成龙是我最喜欢的功夫明星。记得成龙在美国拍 _____ 的时候，他还被国外演员当成了 _____。

 有这样的事？

 有些美国人不知道 _____ 在哪里，在他们眼里 _____ 长得都差不多，再都穿 _____，根本分不出来。

 怪不得近些年成龙经常穿 _____ 呢！久而久之，大家就知道他是 _____ 了。

对话二 Dialogue 2

标志　撞衫　特别　中国人

 有朋，听说成龙喜欢穿唐装，是因为他想让外国人知道他是 _____。

是啊。成龙说穿上唐装，就不用担心和别人 _____ 了。

 近些年唐装几乎成为成龙的 _____ 了。穿唐装的成龙，永远是很 _____ 的。

成龙真是有一颗爱国心！

课后文化实践 Cultural Practice

👤 个人活动　Individual Activity

许多海外华人喜爱穿唐装出席重大活动，请你查找资料，记录几个有代表性的实例，并总结一下这些唐装的特点，下次课给大家介绍。

你为什么喜爱唐装?	唐装的特点
1.	
2.	
3.	
4.	

中国功夫 Chinese *Kung Fu*

中国功夫即中国传统武术，以技击为主要内容，是通过套路搏斗等形式来增强体质、培养意志的民族传统体育项目，也是中华民族智慧的结晶和中华传统文化的体现。中国功夫讲究刚柔并济、内外兼修，内容丰富，流派众多，蕴含着中国人对生命和宇宙的参悟，是中国人长期积累起来的宝贵文化遗产。中国功夫在世界上影响广泛，不仅出现了大量关于中国功夫题材的中外影视作品，更有少林、太极、咏春拳等流派在全球广泛传扬。

Chinese *Kung Fu* is also known as traditional Chinese martial art. *Kung Fu* refers to traditional forms of sport of China as well as a Chinese system of fighting without weapons to bulid up the body and cultivate willpower. *Kung Fu* is a crystallization of Chinese people's wisdom and the embodiment of traditional Chinese culture. Chinese *Kung Fu* emphasises the coupling of force and mercy as well as the combination of internal and external cultivation, which has rich contents and various schools. A reflection of ancient philosophical ideas of life and the universe, *Kung Fu* is a precious cultural heritage formed through long-term accumulation. Chinese *Kung Fu* has a world-wide impact and appears in an array of films and TV productions both home and abroad. Many schools of *Kung Fu* enjoy international popularity, such as Shaolin, Taichi and Yongchun Boxing.

香港 **Hong Kong**

　　香港全称是中华人民共和国香港特别行政区，简称"港"。位于中国南部、珠江口以东，西与中国澳门隔海相望，北与深圳市相邻，南临珠海市万山群岛，区域范围包括香港岛、九龙、新界和周围 262 个岛屿。香港属于亚热带气候，冬季气温可降至 10 摄氏度以下，夏季气温则升至 31 摄氏度以上。香港的秋季天气晴朗，和暖干爽；冬季天气稍冷而且干燥；春季天气温暖潮湿；夏季天气炎热而多雨。香港在 2019 年年中约有 751 万人口，其中绝大部分为华人。香港是世界上人口密度最高的城市之一。

　　Hong Kong is officially known as the Hong Kong Special Administrative Region ("Gang" for short in Chinese). Located in southern China, Hong Kong sits east to the Pearl River Estuary and west to Macau across the South China Sea, while serving as a gateway between Shenzhen on the north and Wanshan Islands of Zhujiang to the south. Its municipality covers Hong Kong Island, Kowloon, New Territories and 262 islands in the periphery. Hong Kong enjoys a subtropical climate. In winter, the temperature can drop below 10℃. And in summer, the temperature can rise above 31℃. The weather in Hong Kong is sunny, warm and dry in autumn; slightly cold and dry in winter; warm and humid in spring and hot and rainy in summer. In mid-2019, Hong kong had a population of about 7.51 million, most of whom were Chinese. Hong Kong is one of the most densely populated cities in the world.

单元自评
Self-Assessment

本单元我们学习了有关中国"服饰文化"的中文表达和文化知识。请你用下面的表格检查一下自己的学习成果吧！如果 5 个中国结是满分，你会给自己几个呢？In this unit, we have learned expressions and cultural knowledge about *Culture in Costume*. Please make use of the table below to evaluate your learning. If five Chinese knots mean full completion, how many will you give yourself?

第7课		🎴	🎴🎴	🎴🎴🎴	🎴🎴🎴🎴	🎴🎴🎴🎴🎴
我会使用下列句型。	·……，即……					
	·……是由……制作而成。					
我知道下列中国文化知识。	·中山装					
	·礼义廉耻					
我了解中山装的特点。						
第8课		🎴	🎴🎴	🎴🎴🎴	🎴🎴🎴🎴	🎴🎴🎴🎴🎴
我会使用下列句型。	·……以……为主					
	·……是……的一个显著特点					
我知道下列中国文化知识。	·旗袍					
	·宋氏三姐妹					
我能为我的朋友介绍旗袍的特点。						
第9课		🎴	🎴🎴	🎴🎴🎴	🎴🎴🎴🎴	🎴🎴🎴🎴🎴
我会使用下列句型。	·被……当成……					
	·……变成/是……的标志					
我知道下列中国文化知识。	·中国功夫					
	·香港					
我能为我的朋友介绍唐装的特点。						

扩展 Further Extension

关于中国"服饰文化"，我还了解以下内容：

1. _____

2. _____

第四单元
UNIT ④

休闲文化
Culture in Leisure

第10课
Lesson 10

Wéiqí yǔ Lànkē Shān
围棋与烂柯山

热身活动 Warm Up

1. 请说说唐装有什么特点。
2. 你会下围棋吗? 你知道围棋的别称吗?

课文 Text

围棋古称为"弈",究竟起源于什么年代,说法有别。据"尧舜以棋教子"的说法,夏商之前就有围棋了。有人认为尧舜处于原始社会末期,创造出如此复杂的科学、艺术和竞技为一体的围棋是有困难的。所以大多认为围棋起源于西周,春秋战国时期已在社会上广泛流行。

围棋又称为"烂柯",这与一个传说有关。烂柯山位于浙江省衢州市东南约十千米处,被誉为"围棋仙地"。传说晋朝时,有一个叫王质的青年到烂柯山砍柴,见山洞内两个童子对弈,便把砍柴的斧子放下,坐在他们身边观阵。直到太阳西斜,一盘棋还没下完。王质本想向童子请教棋艺,突然童子不见了。王质想起自己也该回家了,他回头一看,斧子的把柄已经腐烂。当他再走出山洞,看到一切已面目皆非,一路打听回到村里,因为过去了很久,村里的人都不认识他了。此后,"烂柯"就成了围棋的别称。

(摘编自《围棋与烂柯山》,有删改)

生 词 Words and Expressions

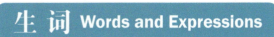

1.	古称	gǔ chēng	be known in ancient times as
2.	究竟	jiūjìng	exactly, on earth
3.	年代	niándài	era, year
4.	原始社会	yuánshǐ shèhuì	primitive society
5.	末期	mòqī	final phase
6.	创造	chuàngzào	create
7.	如此	rúcǐ	so, such
8.	复杂	fùzá	complex
9.	竞技	jìngjì	competition
10.	一体	yìtǐ	unity
11.	困难	kùnnan	difficulty
12.	起源	qǐyuán	originate
13.	时期	shíqī	era, period
14.	广泛	guǎngfàn	widely
15.	青年	qīngnián	youth
16.	砍柴	kǎnchái	cut down trees for firewood
17.	山洞	shāndòng	mountain cave
18.	童子	tóngzǐ	young lad
19.	斧子	fǔzi	axe
20.	观阵	guān zhèn	observe a game of chess
21.	西斜	xī xié	(of the sun) set in the west
22.	请教	qǐngjiào	consult
23.	棋艺	qíyì	board game skill
24.	把柄	bǎbǐng	handle
25.	腐烂	fǔlàn	rot
26.	面目皆非	miànmù jiē fēi	beyond recognition
27.	打听	dǎting	ask about
28.	此后	cǐhòu	afterwards

文化词语

Cultural Words

1.	围棋	wéiqí	go, a type of board game played with black and white pieces on a square wooden board
2.	弈	yì	the ancient name of go
3.	尧	Yáo	Emperor Yao, legendary sage-king in remote antiquity of China
4.	舜	Shùn	Emperor Shun, legendary sage-king in remote antiquity of China
5.	烂柯	Lànkē	namely "rotting axe", another name for go
6.	浙江省	Zhèjiāng shěng	Zhejiang Province
7.	衢州市	Qúzhōu shì	Quzhou City in Zhejiang Province
8.	晋朝	Jìncháo	Jin Dynasty (265–420)
9.	对弈	duìyì	play go

课文理解练习 Text Comprehension

 根据课文选一选 Choose the Right Answers Based on the Text

1. 围棋究竟起源于什么年代，说法有别。据"尧舜以棋教子"的说法，什么时候就有围棋了？

   A 西周　　B 春秋战国　　C 夏商之前　　D 晋朝

2. 樵夫王质从两个童子对弈的山洞里回村后，发生了什么？

   A 斧子的把柄没有腐烂。

   B 一切并没有变化。

   C 所见的人都不认识他了。

   D 童子的一盘棋下完了。

根据提示说一说 Complete the Sentences Based on the Given Clues

1. **所以大多认为围棋起源于西周，春秋战国时期已在社会上广泛流行。**

……**起源于**……

❶ 丝绸之路 _____。（西汉时期）

❷ 儒家思想 _____。（春秋时期）

❸ 印刷术 _____。（中国）

❹ 中山装 _____。（20世纪初期的中国）

2. **此后，"烂柯"就成了围棋的别称。**

（什么）+ **成了** +（什么）+ **的别称**

❶ 紫禁城 _____。（故宫）

❷ 烂柯 _____。（围棋）

❸ 婵娟 _____。（月亮）

❹ 华夏 _____。（中国）

小词库 Word Bank

• 婵娟 chánjuān **the moon**

文化理解练习 Cultural Reading Comprehension

 ### 读一读，想一想 Read and Think

1. 我是伊人。今天我读了"烂柯"的故事。故事说，王质砍柴时看到山洞里有两名童子对弈，便坐下观阵，回家的时候竟然发现自己的斧子柄都腐烂了，村子里的人也都不认识他了。这个传说让我觉得围棋不仅历史悠久，而且还有几分神秘色彩呢！

❓ "烂柯"的故事告诉了我们什么？

Ⓐ 王质的棋艺很好。

Ⓑ 王质不喜欢砍柴。

Ⓒ 王质观棋的时候，世间并没有什么变化。

Ⓓ 王质观棋的时候，时间过了很久很久。

2. 我是有朋。我很喜欢下围棋。爷爷告诉我，下围棋的时候输赢并不是最重要的，重要的是怀着一颗平常心去走好每一步棋，享受下棋的过程，和对手达到棋局上的和谐，围棋中蕴含着中国智慧。

❓ 有朋的爷爷认为下围棋最重要的是什么？

A 局棋的输赢。

B 是否击败了对手。

C 和对手达到棋局上的和谐。

D 不断提高自己的棋艺。

课堂文化交际 Cultural Communication

👥 **小组活动** Group Activity

选词填空，完成对话。再两人一组练习对话。

❙ 对话一 Dialogue 1

春秋战国　夏商　西周　弈

 大龙，你了解围棋吗？

我知道围棋古称为 _____。据"尧舜以棋教子"的说法，_____ 之前就有围棋了。

 是的。但是还有一种说法，认为围棋起源于 _____，_____ 时期已在社会上广泛流行。

围棋的历史真悠久！中国的朝代也真复杂啊！

对话二 Dialogue 2

> 王质　晋朝　面目皆非　烂柯　烂柯山

伊人，你听说过关于围棋的传说吗？

听过。_____ 时，樵夫 _____ 去 _____ 砍柴，看到山洞里两个童子对弈，他就坐下观阵。

对！就是这个传说！传说的后半部分你还记得吗？

记得。后来，两个童子突然不见了，斧子的把柄已经腐烂。王质走出山洞，看到一切已经 _____ 了，他回到村里，村里的人也都不认识他了。

对！所以围棋又叫 _____。

课后文化实践 Cultural Practice

👤 个人活动 Individual Activity

今天我们学习了一个关于围棋的传说，历史上还有许多和围棋相关的故事，请你查找资料，找到和围棋相关的故事，下次课给大家讲一讲。

与围棋有关的故事		
时间	人物	故事情节

围棋 Go (*Weiqi*)

围棋起源于中国，中国古时称之为"弈"，这是一种两人棋类游戏，属琴棋书画四艺之一。战国时已有关于围棋的文字记载。南北朝时期，围棋传入朝鲜半岛、日本，后又流传到欧美。围棋蕴含着中华文化的丰富内涵，它是中国文化与文明的体现。围棋使用方形格状棋盘及黑白二色圆形棋子进行对弈，棋盘上有纵横各 19 道将棋盘分成 361 个交叉点，棋子走在交叉点上，双方交替行棋，每次只能下一子，落子后不能移动，以占据位数多者为胜。围棋被认为是世界上最复杂的棋盘游戏之一。

A board game for two players, go (*weiqi*) originated from China and was called "*yi* (弈)" in ancient times. It is one of the Four Arts together with lyre-playing, calligraphy and painting. There were written records of go as early as the Warring States Period. Back in the Southern and Northern Dynasties, go spread to the Korean Peninsula, Japan and finally reached Europe and America. Go contains rich Chinese cultural contents and is a representation of Chinese civilisation. The game go uses a 19-by-19-line square board with 361 intersecting points and round black and white pieces (called "stones"). Players take turns placing a stone once on vacant points on the board to surround the opponents' stones to form territories. Once placed, stones are not moved. The player with the larger amount of occupied points is the winner. Go is considered one of the most complex board games in the world.

尧、舜、禹 Emperor Yao, Emperor Shun and Emperor Yu

尧、舜、禹是古代中国传说中在黄河流域先后出现的三位德才兼备的部落联盟首领。尧曾将帝位让位给舜，舜将帝位让位给禹。据记载，尧舜之时，发生滔天洪水，禹以天下为己任，率领百姓疏通江河，治理水患，发展农业。传说禹为了治水曾"三过家门而不入"。禹完成治水大业后，天下安宁祥和，建立了夏朝。

Emperor Yao, Emperor Shun, and Emperor Yu, who have both ability and political integrity, are three tribal leaders in the Yellow River Basin in ancient Chinese legends. Emperor Yao abdicated the throne to Emperor Shun, and Emperor Shun abdicated the throne to Emperor Yu. According to records, there was a huge flood during the reign of Emperor Yao and Emperor Shun. Emperor Yu took the world as his own responsibility leading the people to dredge the river, control the flood, and develop agriculture. Legend has it that Emperor Yu once "passed home three times but did not enter" in order to control the flood. After Emperor Yu completed the great cause of water control, the world was peaceful and the Xia Dynasty was then established.

11

第11课
Lesson 11

Fàng fēngzheng
放 风 筝

课文 Text

　　我对放风筝有特殊的癖好，从孩提时起直到三四十岁，遇有机会从没有放弃过这一有趣的游戏。在北平（今北京），放风筝有一定的季节，大约总是在新年过后开春的时候为宜。这时，风劲且稳。严冬时风很大，过于凶猛；春季过后则风又嫌微弱了。开春的时候，风不断地吹，最好放风筝。

　　北平的风筝最考究。因为北平的有闲阶级的人多，如八旗子弟。我家住在东城，东四南大街，在内务部街与史家胡同之间有一个二郎庙，庙旁边有一个风筝铺，铺主姓于，人称"风筝于"。他做的风筝，种类繁多，如肥沙燕、瘦沙燕、龙井鱼、蝴蝶、蜻蜓、鲇鱼、灯笼、白菜、蜈蚣、美人、八卦、蛤蟆，以及其他形形色色的。鱼的眼睛是活动的，放起来滴溜溜地转，尾巴拖得很长，临风波动。蝴蝶、蜻蜓的翅膀也有软的，波动起来也很好看。

　　我以为放风筝是一件颇有情趣的事。人在世上，局处在一个小圈圈里，大概没有不想偶尔远走高飞一下的。出门旅行，游山玩水，是一个办法，然亦不可常得。放风筝时，看风筝冉冉上升，然后停在高空，这时仿佛自己也跟着风筝飞起了，俯瞰尘寰，怡然自得。

（摘编自《放风筝》，有删改）

生词 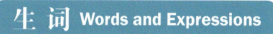Words and Expressions

1.	癖好	pǐhào	hobby, fetish
2.	孩提	háití	childhood
3.	游戏	yóuxì	game
4.	季节	jìjié	season
5.	开春	kāichūn	the beginning of spring
6.	劲	jìn	strong
7.	稳	wěn	stable
8.	严冬	yándōng	severe winter
9.	凶猛	xiōngměng	ferocious
10.	微弱	wēiruò	weak
11.	考究	kǎojiu	exquisite
12.	有闲	yǒu xián	(of people) have much leisure time, not occupied by work
13.	阶级	jiējí	class, social stratum
14.	铺	pù	shop
15.	种类繁多	zhǒnglèi fánduō	various, diverse
16.	沙燕	shāyàn	bank swallow
17.	龙井鱼	lóngjǐng yú	dragon-eyed goldfish
18.	蝴蝶	húdié	butterfly
19.	蜻蜓	qīngtíng	dragonfly
20.	鲇鱼	niányú	catfish
21.	灯笼	dēnglong	lantern

22.	白菜	báicài	Chinese cabbage, pak choi
23.	蜈蚣	wúgōng	centipede
24.	美人	měirén	beauty
25.	蛤蟆	háma	frog, toad
26.	形形色色	xíngxing sèsè	of all forms
27.	滴溜溜	dīliūliū	motion of rolling or flowing
28.	尾巴	wěiba	tail
29.	翅膀	chìbǎng	wing
30.	波动	bōdòng	fluctuate
31.	情趣	qíngqù	joy
32.	偶然	ǒurán	occasionally
33.	远走高飞	yuǎnzǒu gāofēi	travel to faraway places
34.	游山玩水	yóushān wánshuǐ	travel to mountains and rivers, travel extensively
35.	冉冉上升	rǎnrǎn shàngshēng	rise gradually
36.	高空	gāokōng	high in the sky
37.	仿佛	fǎngfú	as if
38.	俯瞰	fǔkàn	overlook
39.	尘寰	chénhuán	the universe, the world
40.	怡然自得	yírán zìdé	enjoy oneself

文化词语
Cultural Words

1.	北平	Běipíng	the old name of Beijing
2.	八旗子弟	bāqí zǐdì	children of the Eight Banners
3.	东城	Dōngchéng	Dongcheng District
4.	东四南大街	Dōngsì Nán Dàjiē	Dongsi South Avenue
5.	内务部街	Nèiwùbù Jiē	Neiwubu Street
6.	史家胡同	Shǐjiā Hútòng	Shijia Hutong
7.	二郎庙	Èrláng Miào	Erlang Temple
8.	八卦	bāguà	Eight Trigrams

课文理解练习 Text Comprehension

根据课文选一选 Choose the Right Answers Based on the Text

1. 在北平（今北京），什么时候放风筝为宜？

   A 严冬的时候　　B 严冬之前　　C 春季之后　　D 开春的时候

2. "眼睛是活动的，放起来滴溜溜地转"的是哪种风筝？

A 鱼形风筝

B 蝴蝶风筝

C 蜻蜓风筝

D 沙燕风筝

💬 **根据提示说一说** Complete the Sentences Based on the Given Clues

1. （我）**从**孩提时**起直到**三四十岁，遇有机会从没有
放弃过这一有趣的游戏。

> 从……起直到……

❶ _____ ，京剧一直比较受欢迎。（清朝末期、现在）

❷ _____ ，旗袍一直很受中国女性的喜爱。（20世纪初、现在）

❸ 我 _____ ，每年春天都会和朋友一起放风筝。（孩提时、现在）

❹ _____ ，天安门广场始终有很多游客。（凌晨、深夜）

2. **在**内务部街与史家胡同**之间有**一个二郎庙。

> 在……+ 之间有 +（什么）

❶ 乾清宫　　坤宁宫　　交泰殿

❷ 珠海　　香港　　澳门　　港珠澳大桥

❸ 昆明湖的两岸　　十七孔桥

❹ 中国古代建筑的单体　　单体　　廊

文化理解练习 Cultural Reading Comprehension

 读一读，选一选 Read and Choose

1. 我是李晶，我和小伙伴特别喜欢放风筝。你知道
吗，放风筝还有时节的讲究呢，最好的时节是新年
过后开春的时候，因为这时风劲且稳，风筝很容易
就可以飞上天。严冬时风很大，过于凶猛；春天过
后风又比较弱了，不利于放风筝。

> **小词库 Word Bank**
>
> • 时节 shíjié season

❓ 李晶认为什么时节放风筝最好？

🅰 端午节的时候　🅱 放暑假的时候　🅲 立冬的时候　🅳 开春的时候

2. 我是大龙。今天我和伊人去公园放风筝，在公园里，我看到了很多种类的风筝，有波动起来非常好看的软翅风筝，比如蝴蝶风筝和蜻蜓风筝；还有以蜈蚣风筝为代表的串式风筝，它飞上天的时候壮观极了；最具特色的是沙燕风筝，它的颜色很丰富，图案也很生动，活灵活现，惹人喜爱。

小词库 Word Bank

- 壮观　　　zhuàngguān　　magnificent
- 生动　　　shēngdòng　　　vivid
- 活灵活现　huólíng huóxiàn　lively
- 惹人喜爱　rěrén xǐ'ài　　　adorable

如果大龙和伊人放的是串式风筝，那么他们的风筝应该是以下哪个？

Ａ 蝴蝶风筝　Ｂ 蜻蜓风筝　Ｃ 蜈蚣风筝　Ｄ 沙燕风筝

课堂文化交际 Cultural Communication

 小组活动 Group Activity

选词填空，完成对话。再两人一组练习对话。

对话一 Dialogue 1

开春　三四十岁　严冬　微弱　劲　稳　孩提

 中国著名作家梁实秋很喜欢放风筝，他从 _____ 时起一直到 _____，都很热爱这个有趣的游戏。

是啊！大龙，我考考你，你知道在北京哪个季节最适合放风筝吗？

 我当然知道了！放风筝在新年过后 _____ 的时候最为宜。因为这时候，风 _____ 且 _____。

你说得对！_____ 时风很大，过于凶猛；春季过后风又嫌 _____ 了。所以开春是放风筝最好的季节。

对话二 Dialogue 2

情趣　滴溜溜　有闲阶级　蜻蜓　怡然自得　风筝　种类繁多

北平（今北京）的 _____ 最考究。因为当时北平的 _____ 的人多。

听说当时的风筝 _____，很有趣。

我最喜欢鱼形的风筝，它被放起来的时候眼睛 _____ 地转，尾巴还能临风波动。

蝴蝶、_____ 风筝也很有趣，它们有软软的翅膀，波动起来很好看。

放风筝是件有 _____ 的事，看着风筝冉冉上升，心情一定是 _____ 的！

课后文化实践 Cultural Practice

👤 个人活动 Individual Activity

2008 年北京奥运会的吉祥物福娃中的"妮妮"，就是以沙燕风筝为原型塑造的。沙燕风筝有哪些特点和寓意能让它成为福娃"妮妮"的灵感来源？请查找相关资料，下次课给大家讲讲。

特点	寓意

北平 **Beiping**

　　北平，简称"平"，是北京在历史上曾经使用的名称之一。明朝洪武元年（1368 年）"大都"更名为"北平府"，取"北方安宁平定"之意，"北平"第一次成为北京的名称。后于明朝永乐十九年（1421 年）作为明朝的都城改名为"北京"，此为今名之始。民国十七年（1928 年）设立"北平特别市"，相当于今日的直辖市。1949 年 9 月 21 日，中国人民政治协商会议第一届全国委员会全体会议在北平市中南海怀仁堂隆重开幕。会议通过了中华人民共和国首都设于"北平市"，同时将"北平市"改名为"北京市"。

"Beiping (北平)", or "Ping (平)" for short, is one of the historical names of Beijing. In the first year of Emperor Hongwu's reign in the Ming Dynasty (1368), "Dadu" (大都, Great Capital) city was renamed "Beiping Fu" for its auspicious meaning of "peace in the north". That was when the area was first referred to as "Beiping". Later in the 19th year of Emperor Yongle's reign in the Ming Dynasty (1421), the area was renamed "Beijing" (北京, Capital City in the North). In the 17th year of the Republic of China (1928), the government set up "Beiping Special City", an equivalent to the present-day municipality directly under the Central Government. On September 21st 1949, the first plenary session of the Chinese People's Political Consultative Conference was held in Huairen Hall, Zhongnanhai, Beiping. The city was chosen to be the site for the capital of the People's Republic of China and was finally renamed "Beijing" as we know it today.

八旗子弟 Children of the Eight Banners

八旗子弟指八旗旗人，八旗制度终结后，多指八旗旗人的后人。八旗制度是清代满族的一种社会组织形式，以旗为号，分为正黄、正白、正红、正蓝、镶黄、镶白、镶红、镶蓝八旗。各旗当中因族源不同又分为八旗满洲、八旗蒙古和八旗汉军。满洲、蒙古、汉军同属一旗，旗色亦相同，只是从军、入仕待遇略有不同。

"Children of the Eight Banners" originally referred to the clansmen of the Eight Banners ("Baqi", the Banner system). After the Banner system was abolished, the term was often used to refer to Baqi descendants. Baqi was the social system used by the Manchu people in the Qing Dynasty. The Eight Banners were "Zhenghuangqi (Plain Yellow Banner)", "Zhengbaiqi (Plain White Banner)", "Zhenghongqi (Plain Red Banner)", "Zhenglanqi (Plain Blue Banner)", "Xianghuangqi (Bordered Yellow Banner)", "Xiangbaiqi (Bordered White Banner)", "Xianghongqi (Bordered Red Banner)", and "Xianglanqi (Bordered Blue Banner)". On ethnic grounds, each banner was further categorised into Manchu, Mongol and Hanjun Baqi, who shared the banner colours but differed slightly in pay levels as army men and civil servants.

12

第12课
Lesson 12

Tī jiànzi
踢毽子

热身活动 Warm Up

1. 请给大家说说沙燕风筝的特点和寓意。
2. 你踢过毽子吗？你知道毽子有哪些踢法吗？

课文 Text

　　我们小时候踢毽子，毽子都是自己做的。选两个小钱（制钱），叠在一起，用布缝实，这便是毽子托。在毽托一面，缝一截鹅毛管，在鹅毛管中插入鸡毛，便是一只毽子。

　　我们那里毽子的踢法很复杂，花样很多。有小五套、中五套、大五套。小五套是"扬、拐、尖、托、笃"，是用右脚的不同部位踢的。中五套是"偷、跳、舞、环、踩"，也是用右脚踢，同时以左脚做不同的姿势来配合。大五套则是同时运用两脚踢，分"对、岔、绕、掼、挝"。小五套技术比较简单，运动量较小，一般是女生踢的；中五套较难；大五套则难度很大，运动量也很大。

　　踢毽子是孩子的事，偶尔见到近二十边上的人还踢，少。北京则有老人踢毽子。有一年，下大雪，大清早，我去逛天坛，在天坛门洞里见到几位老人踢毽子。他们之中，最年轻的也有六十多了。他们轮流传递着踢，一个传给一个，那个接过来，踢一两下，传给另一个。"脚法"大都是"扬"，间或也来一下"跳"。我在旁边也看了五分钟，毽子始终没有落到地上。他们大概是"毽友"，经常，也许是每天在一起踢。老人都腿脚利落，身板挺直，面色红润，双眼有光。大雪天，这几位老人像是一幅画，一首诗。

（摘编自《踢毽子》，有删改）

生 词 Words and Expressions

1.	叠	dié	overlap, put one thing on top of another
2.	缝	féng	sew
3.	一截	yì jié	a length of
4.	鹅毛	émáo	goose feather
5.	鸡毛	jīmáo	chicken feather
6.	踢法	tīfǎ	kicking technique
7.	花样	huāyàng	variety
8.	扬	yáng	throw up, kick the shuttlecock with the toes of the right foot
9.	拐	guǎi	turn, bend the right knee sideways and kick the shuttlecock with the outer side of the right foot
10.	笃	dǔ	kick the shuttlecock with the inner side of the heel of the right foot
11.	部位	bùwèi	part
12.	偷	tōu	stand on one foot and kick the shuttlecock with the other foot behind the body
13.	踩	cǎi	step on
14.	姿势	zīshì	posture
15.	配合	pèihé	co-operation
16.	掼	guàn	toss
17.	技术	jìshù	technique, skill
18.	简单	jiǎndān	simple
19.	运动量	yùndòng liàng	amount of physical exercise
20.	门洞	méndòng	doorway, gateway
21.	轮流	lúnliú	take turns
22.	传递	chuándì	pass on
23.	间或	jiànhuò	occasionally, once in a while
24.	腿脚	tuǐjiǎo	leg and foot, ability to walk
25.	利落	lìluo	agile
26.	身板	shēnbǎn	body, figure
27.	面色	miànsè	complexion
28.	红润	hóngrùn	ruddy

文化词语
Cultural Words

1. 毽子   jiànzi   shuttlecock, a traditional Chinese game, in which players try to keep a weighted shuttlecock in the air by kicking
2. 小钱   xiǎo qián   holed copper coin
3. 毽子托   jiànzi tuō   the weighted base of a shuttlecock
4. 毽友   jiànyǒu   shuttlecock friends, people who play shuttlecock together

课文理解练习 Text Comprehension

 根据课文选一选 Choose the Right Answers Based on the Text

1. 毽子托是用什么材料制作的？

A
小钱

B
鹅毛管

C 
鸡毛

D 
鸭毛

2. 下列属于毽子的"中五套"踢法的是？

A 扬、拐、尖、托、笃   B 偷、跳、舞、环、踩

C 对、岔、绕、掼、挝   D 用右脚的不同部位踢

💬 **根据提示说一说** Complete the Sentences Based on the Given Clues

1. 他们之中，最年轻的也有六十多了。   ……之中，最……有/是……

❶ 中国的河流 ＿＿＿＿＿＿＿＿。（长，长江）

❷ 网师园 ＿＿＿＿＿＿＿＿。（有名的景点，月到风来亭）

❸ 京剧旦角 ＿＿＿＿＿＿＿＿。（著名的演员，梅兰芳）

❹ 苏州美景 ＿＿＿＿＿＿＿＿。（有代表性的，苏州园林）

小词库 Word Bank

- 梅兰芳　Méi Lánfāng　Mei Lanfang (1864–1961), a famed Beijing opera artist

2. "脚法"**大都**是"扬"，**间或**也来一下"跳"。　｜……**大都**……，**间或**……

① 夏天的傍晚，坐卧在上海的弄堂里的 ＿＿＿＿＿＿＿。（老人，年轻人）

② 北京街道 ＿＿＿＿＿＿＿。（正南正北、正东正西，斜的）

③ 北京的胡同里 ＿＿＿＿＿＿＿。（店铺，名人故居）

④ 参观敦煌莫高窟的人 ＿＿＿＿＿＿＿。（游客，研究文物的学者）

文化理解练习 Cultural Reading Comprehension

 读一读，选一选 Read and Choose

1. 我是有朋，我来为你介绍三套毽子的踢法，分别是：小五套、中五套和大五套。小五套是"扬、拐、尖、托、笃"，用右脚的不同部位踢，技术比较简单，运动量较小，一般是女生踢的。中五套是"偷、跳、舞、环、踩"，也是用右脚踢，同时以左脚做不同的姿势来配合。大五套则是同时运用两脚踢，分为"对、岔、绕、掼、挝"，难度很大。你想不想尝试一下呢？

❓ 下列哪一项在描述"小五套"的踢法？

Ａ 用右脚的不同部位踢，技术比较简单，运动量较小。

Ｂ 偷、跳、舞、环、踩。

Ｃ 左脚和右脚配合着踢。

Ｄ 同时运用两脚踢，难度比较大。

2. 我是伊人，我觉得踢毽子既有趣味性，又可以锻炼身体，是一项很有意义的运动。踢毽子没有年龄的限制，小朋友和老年人都可以踢。踢毽子可以提高人的反应能力，锻炼专注力，而且踢毽子能够活动肌肉，一抬一跳都需要身体各部分的协调，对身体非常有益。

❓ 下列关于踢毽子的叙述，错误的一项是？

A 踢毽子是一项有趣味性的运动。

B 老年人和小朋友都可以踢毽子。

C 踢毽子可以提高人的反应能力。

D 踢毽子不一定对身体有益。

小词库 Word Bank

- 锻炼　　　duànliàn　　　strengthen
- 限制　　　xiànzhì　　　restriction
- 反应能力　fǎnyìng nénglì　reaction
- 专注力　　zhuānzhùlì　　concentration
- 活动肌肉　huódòng jīròu　exercise the muscles
- 协调　　　xiétiáo　　　coordination

课堂文化交际 Cultural Communication

 小组活动　Group Activity

选词填空，完成对话。再两人一组练习对话。

对话一 Dialogue 1

托　笃　运动量　大五套　左脚　跳　环　中五套　掼　挞　尖

 伊人，你知道毽子的三套踢法吗？

 我喜欢踢毽子，当然知道了！毽子的三种踢法是小五套、＿＿＿＿＿和＿＿＿＿＿。

 我今天才弄清楚，小五套是指"扬、拐、＿＿＿＿＿、＿＿＿＿＿、笃"，是用右脚的不同部位踢的。

你说得对！中五套是"偷、_____、舞、_____、踩"，也是用右脚踢，用 _____ 作不同的姿势配合。

你还真是这方面的专家呢！大五套是"对、岔、绕、_____、_____"，难度很大，_____ 也比较大。

踢毽子是项有趣的运动，走，咱俩去踢毽子吧！

▍对话二 Dialogue 2

传递　扬　跳　利落　红润　毽友　天坛

有朋，我在公园里经常看见一些老年人围在一起踢毽子。没想到这项运动在中国这么受欢迎啊！

中国作家汪曾祺在散文《踢毽子》中曾写过中国老年人在 _____ 门洞里踢毽子的情景，他们轮流 _____ 着踢，一个传给一个，脚法大都是"_____"，也有"_____"，技术很好。

他们大概是"_____"，可能每天都在一起踢毽子。

汪曾祺先生曾经这样写道：老人们都腿脚 _____，身板挺直，面色 _____，双眼有光，真像是一幅画、一首诗。

课后文化实践 Cultural Practice

 个人活动 Individual Activity

你的国家有什么有趣的休闲方式或者特别的娱乐项目？它们有什么特点？下节课给大家讲讲！

我们国家的休闲娱乐方式		
1	**2**	**3**
特点	特点	特点

小钱（制钱）**The Standard Copper Coins**

小钱是铜钱最普通的形制，即一文小钱，又称平钱，它是使用铜钱时代的最小货币单位，其直径约 2.4—2.5 厘米，重约 3—4 克。明清两代按其当朝法定的钱币体制由官炉铸行钱币，以别于前朝旧钱和本朝的私铸钱，并对旧钱、私铸钱进行取缔和制约。清代制钱基本形制仍为圆形方孔。钱文正面铸有"某朝通宝"字样，咸丰以后有改铸"某朝重宝""某朝元宝"。

The standard copper coin is a penny of copper coins. Measuring 2.4 – 2.5 centimetres in diametre and 3 – 4 grams in weight, it is the smallest currency unit back in the copper money era. During the Ming and Qing Dynasties, national mints followed their respective currency systems to distinguish official money from illegally minted money and old money made in previous dynasties, which were in turn abolished and regulated. Qing Dynasty's coins were primarily round with square holes in the centre and inscribed on the head with the legend "... Dynasty's Tongbao" and later changed to "... Dynasty's Zhongbao (重宝)", "... Dynasty's Yuanbao (元宝)" since Emperor Xianfeng's reign.

天坛　The Temple of Heaven

　　天坛是世界上最大的古代祭天建筑群，位于北京市南部，占地约273万平方米。天坛始建于明永乐十八年（1420年），明清时曾重修改建，为明清两代皇帝"祭天""祈谷"的场所。天坛有坛墙两重，形成内坛和外坛两部分，坛墙南方北圆，象征天圆地方。主要建筑集中在内坛，圜丘坛在南、祈谷坛在北，二坛同在一条南北轴线上，中间有墙相隔。圜丘坛内主要建筑有圜丘坛、皇穹宇等，祈谷坛内主要建筑有祈年殿、皇乾殿、祈年门等。

　　The Temple of Heaven is the largest buildings for worship of heaven. Situated in southern Beijing, the Temple of Heaven stretches an area of 2,730,000 square metres. First built in the 18th year of the reign of Emperor Yongle in the Ming Dynasty (1420), the Temple of Heaven was expanded and reconstructed during the reign of Ming and Qing Dynasties. The Temple of Heaven served as the site for Ming and Qing emperors to conduct rites of sacrifice and praying. Divided by two encircling walls into an inner part and an outer part, the Temple of Heaven consists of two main buildings separated by a wall in the inner part along the central axis — Yuanqiu (圜丘) at the south end and Qigu (祈谷) at the north end. The northern part within the walls is semicircular symbolising the heavens and the southern part is square symbolising the earth, a design that reflects the ancient Chinese thought of "the heaven is round and the earth is square". Yuanqiu is mainly comprised of the Circular Mound Altar and the Imperial Vault of Heaven, while Qigu primarily contains the Hall of Prayer for Good Harvest, the Hall of Imperial Zenith, and the Gate of Prayer for Good Harvest.

单元自评
Self-Assessment

本单元我们学习了有关中国"休闲文化"的中文表达和文化知识。请你用下面的表格检查一下自己的学习成果吧！如果 5 个中国结是满分，你会给自己几个呢？In this unit, we have learned expressions and cultural knowledge about *Culture in Leisure*. Please make use of the table below to evaluate your learning. If five Chinese knots mean full completion, how many will you give yourself?

第10课						
我会使用下列句型。	·……起源于……					
	·（什么）+成了+（什么）+的别称					
我知道下列中国文化知识。	·围棋					
	·尧、舜、禹					
我能说出中国围棋的特点。						
第11课						
我会使用下列句型。	·从……起直到……					
	·在……+之间有+（什么）					
我知道下列中国文化知识。	·北平					
	·八旗子弟					
我能为我的朋友介绍中国风筝的形状。						
第12课						
我会使用下列句型。	·……之中，最……有/是……					
	·……大都……，间或……					
我知道下列中国文化知识。	·小钱（制钱）					
	·天坛					
我能为我的朋友介绍毽子的玩法。						

扩展 Further Extension

关于中国"休闲文化"，我还了解了以下内容：

1. _____

2. _____

第五单元
UNIT ⑤

戏曲文化
Culture in Chinese Opera

第13课
Lesson 13

Guócuì jīngjù
国粹京剧

13

热身活动 Warm Up

1. 请讲讲你们国家的有趣的休闲方式或者娱乐项目。
2. 听歌曲《唱脸谱》，看看你能听出几种脸谱。

课文 Text

梅兰芳是京剧表演艺术大师。他的生动表演诠释了何为京剧之美。娓娓念唱，意味深长。优雅身段，如秋叶静美。一阵锣鼓经，舞台上气势磅礴，轻盈的水袖，起伏的碎步，皆体现京剧手、眼、身、法、步的意境和神韵。

老北京人把看戏又称为听戏，听则听其腔，唱腔或明快，或浑厚，念白节奏铿锵，韵味十足。看则看其身段、扮相，脸谱是扮相的灵魂，表现戏中人物的忠奸善恶、喜怒哀乐。略施脂粉的，是"生角"和"旦角"；重施油彩的，是"净行"；那鼻梁上一抹白粉的，就是俗称小花脸的"丑角"。

京剧，讲究虚化的意境。一根马鞭，代表策马奔腾；一根船桨，就象征着撑船破浪。京剧"无声不歌，无动不舞"，"唱""念"是歌，"做""打"是舞，"唱、念、做、打"包含了京剧的主要精髓。

这就是京剧，一腔开唱，百转回折，一颦一笑，皆是神采。

生 词 New Words and Expressions

1.	表演	biǎoyǎn	performance
2.	诠释	quánshì	interpret
3.	娓娓念唱	wěiwěi niànchàng	recite and sing opera lines elegantly and tirelessly
4.	意味深长	yìwèi shēncháng	with profundity
5.	优雅	yōuyǎ	elegant
6.	静美	jìngměi	solemnly beautiful
7.	气势磅礴	qìshì pángbó	of tremendous momentum
8.	起伏	qǐfú	undulating
9.	意境	yìjìng	artistic concept
10.	神韵	shényùn	charm
11.	明快	míngkuài	light and cheerful
12.	浑厚	húnhòu	(of voice) resonant and deep
13.	铿锵	kēngqiāng	with a strong beat
14.	韵味	yùnwèi	style
15.	灵魂	línghún	soul
16.	忠奸善恶	zhōngjiān shàn'è	the loyal, the treacherous, the good and the evil; all kinds of people
17.	喜怒哀乐	xǐnù āilè	joy, anger, sorrow and happiness; all emotions
18.	略施脂粉	lüèshī zhīfěn	with light make-up
19.	重施油彩	zhòngshī yóucǎi	with heavy make-up
20.	鼻梁	bíliáng	nose bridge
21.	抹	mǒ	measure word for cloud, etc.
22.	白粉	báifěn	white powder
23.	俗称	súchēng	generally known as
24.	虚化	xūhuà	virtual
25.	马鞭	mǎbiān	horsewhip
26.	策马奔腾	cèmǎ bēnténg	whipping and riding the horse
27.	船桨	chuánjiǎng	roar
28.	撑船破浪	chēngchuán pòlàng	rolling the boat and breaking the waves
29.	包含	bāohán	include
30.	精髓	jīngsuí	essence
31.	百转回折	bǎizhuǎn huízhé	(of sound) making various changes in pitch, tune, etc.
32.	颦	pín	frown
33.	神采	shéncǎi	elegant demeanour

文化词语
Cultural Words

1.	国粹	guócuì	quintessence of Chinese culture
2.	京剧	jīngjù	Beijing opera
3.	梅兰芳	Méi Lánfāng	Mei Lanfang (1894–1961), a famed Beijing opera artist
4.	身段	shēnduàn	the graceful bearing of opera performers
5.	锣鼓经	luógǔjīng	a tune played by percussion instruments
6.	水袖	shuǐxiù	water sleeves, double white silk sleeves attached to the cuffs of traditional Chinese opera or dance costumes
7.	碎步	suìbù	a special motion in Beijing opera, to walk with short quick steps
8.	腔	qiāng	melodies for the singing part in a Chinese opera
9.	念白	niànbái	recitation, spoken parts in a Chinese opera
10.	扮相	bànxiàng	stage appearance
11.	脸谱	liǎnpǔ	types of facial makeup indicating personalities and characters in Chinese operas
12.	生角	shēngjué	male characters in Beijing opera
13.	旦角	dànjué	female characters in Beijing opera
14.	净行	jìngháng	male characters with painted faces in Beijing opera, usually virile or with rough character
15.	小花脸	xiǎohuāliǎn	another name for *chou* characters
16.	丑角	chǒujué	comic, villainous or righteous characters in Beijing opera, recognised by the patch of white paint around the eyes and nose

课文理解练习 Text Comprehension

 根据课文选一选 Choose the Right Answers Based on the Text

1. 京剧里鼻梁上一抹白粉的，俗称小花脸的是什么角？

A

生角

B

旦角

C

净行

D

丑角

2. 在京剧中，用什么来象征策马奔腾？

A ☐

一支船桨

B ☐

一匹马

C ☐

一条马鞭

D ☐

一片草原

💬 **根据提示说一说** Complete the Sentences Based on the Given Clues

1. 老北京人**把**看戏又**称为**听戏。　　　把 +（什么）+ 称为 +（什么）

　❶ 在京剧中，我们 ＿＿＿＿＿＿＿。（年轻的女性角色，旦角）

　❷ 人们 ＿＿＿＿＿＿＿。（梅兰芳，京剧表演大师）

　❸ 中国人 ＿＿＿＿＿＿＿。（黄河，母亲河）

　❹ 人们习惯 ＿＿＿＿＿＿＿。（戏班，梨园）

2. 一根船桨，就**象征着**撑船破浪。　　　……**象征着**……

　❶ 在京剧中，马鞭 ＿＿＿＿＿＿＿。（策马奔腾）

　❷ 颐和园东边的文昌阁和西边的宿云檐城关是 ＿＿＿＿＿＿＿。（"文武辅弼"的两座建筑）

　❸ 长城 ＿＿＿＿＿＿＿。（民族精神）

　❹ 月饼是中秋节吃的传统美食，＿＿＿＿＿＿＿。（团圆美满）

文化小词库 Cultural Word Bank

- 文昌阁　　　Wénchāng Gé　　　**Wenchang Tower**
- 宿云檐城关　Sùyúnyán Chéngguān　**Tower of Cloud-Retaining Eaves**

文化理解练习 Cultural Reading Comprehension

 读一读，选一选 Read and Choose

1. 我是大龙，今天我和伊人去大剧院看了一场京剧演出。我了解到在京剧表演中，有唱、念、做、打四种基本功："唱"指唱腔，"念"指念白，"做"指各种形体动作，"打"指武术的技艺。

❓ 在京剧表演中，展示武术技艺的是哪种基本功？

Ⓐ 唱　Ⓑ 念　Ⓒ 做　Ⓓ 打

小词库 Word Bank

- 基本功　jīběngōng basic skills
- 形体　xíngtǐ physique
- 技艺　jìyì skill

2. 我是伊人，上次看完京剧演出后，我对京剧产生了浓厚的兴趣，我查了很多资料，了解到京剧分为生、旦、净、丑四种角色。其中，"生""净"是男性角色；"旦"是女性角色的统称；"丑"角中大都是表现幽默或阴险狡猾的男性角色。

❓ 年轻漂亮的女性属于京剧中的哪种角色？

Ⓐ 生　Ⓑ 旦　Ⓒ 净　Ⓓ 丑

小词库 Word Bank

- 浓厚　nónghòu deep, rich
- 统称　tǒngchēng general term
- 幽默　yōumò humorous
- 阴险狡猾　yīnxiǎn jiǎohuá wicked and cunning

课堂文化交际 Cultural Communication

 小组活动 Group Activity

选词填空，完成对话。再两人一组练习对话。

对话一 Dialogue 1

生　旦　净　丑　京剧　身段　扮相

李晶，你了解京剧吗？京剧我听不太懂。应该如何欣赏京剧呢？

 伊人，京剧的主要精髓包括"唱、念、做、打"。听不懂唱词，依然可以欣赏京剧，因为除了唱腔之外，_____ 和 _____ 也是京剧的重要表现形式。

 你的意思是说京剧是视听结合的艺术？

 对，京剧包括 _____、_____、_____、_____ 四种角色。不仅可以听京剧，还可以看京剧！

对话二 Dialogue 2

丑角　白粉　净行

 有朋，生、旦、净、丑四种京剧扮相中，你最喜欢哪种扮相？

 我最喜欢脸上重施油彩的 _____ 扮相，他们一般身材高大，看着太威风了！大龙，你喜欢哪种扮相？

 我喜欢 _____ 的扮相。鼻梁上一抹 _____，像个小花脸，我觉得太有趣了！

课后文化实践 Cultural Practice

 个人活动　Individual Activity

请找资料，欣赏一段京剧，下次课给同学介绍一下这段京剧的剧名、主要人物和故事内容。

剧名	主要人物	故事内容

京剧 **Beijing Opera**

京剧，是中国影响最大的戏曲剧种，有"国粹"之称。京剧流行全中国，已有 200 多年历史。清代乾隆年间，四大徽班陆续进北京演出，与来自湖北的汉调艺人合作，同时接受了昆曲、秦腔的部分剧目、曲调和表演方法，又吸收了一些地方民间曲调，通过不断的融合，最终形成京剧。经过无数艺人的长期舞台实践，京剧舞台艺术在文学、表演、音乐、唱腔、锣鼓、化妆、脸谱等各个方面，构成了一套互相制约、相得益彰的格律化和规范化的程式。

Beijing opera is the most influential operatic form in China and is extolled as the quintessence of Chinese culture. Beijing opera enjoys nationwide presence and has a history of more than 200 years. During the Qing Emperor Qianlong's reign, the Four Great Anhui Troupes came to Beijing, bringing *Anhui* opera. Cooperating with *Handiao* artists from Hubei, they brought together some repertoires, melodies and performing skills of *kunqu* opera and *Qinqiang* opera, and further combined some local tunes. In the continuing integration of diverse operatic genres, Beijing opera eventually took shape. Through the long-term stage practices of various artists, a paradigm came to be established for the regularisation and normalisation of the operatic literature, performance, music, singing, instruments, make-up, and facial painting, which restrict and complement each other.

梅兰芳 **Mei Lanfang**

梅兰芳，本名梅澜，艺名兰芳，1894 年出生于北京的一个梨园世家，8 岁学艺，11 岁登台，1961 年病逝。梅兰芳演青衣，兼演刀马旦。他在长期的舞台实践中，发展和提高了京剧旦角的表演艺术，形成一个具有独特风格的艺术流派，影响很广，世称"梅派"。梅兰芳曾赴日、美等国进行文化交流，是享有国际盛誉的中国京剧表演艺术大师。其代表作有《贵妃醉酒》《宇宙锋》《霸王别姬》等。

Mei Lanfang, original name Mei Lan, stage name Lanfang, was born into an opera family in Beijing in 1894. He began studying Beijing opera at the age of 8 and made his stage debut at 11 years old. He died in 1961. Mei Lanfang played female role and *daomadan* (actress skilled in acrobatic fighting) in Beijing opera. Through many years of acting, Mei Lanfang enhanced the performance art of *dan* characters in Beijing opera and developed a unique artistic school, which came to be known as the "Mei School" and was popular in China. Mei Lanfang was also an internationally famed maestro of Beijing opera, who has visited Japan, US and other countries. Some of his most representative works are *Guifei Zuijiu* (Drunken Beauty), *Yuzhou Feng* (Blade of Cosmos), and *Farewell! My Concubine*, etc.

Yǎsú–gòngshǎng de
雅俗共赏的
Kūnqǔ
昆曲

课 文 Text

　　曹雪芹的《红楼梦》成书于乾隆年间，正是昆曲鼎盛之时，上至王卿贵族，下至市井小民，对昆曲的热爱，由南到北，举国若狂。苏州是明清两代的昆曲中心，万历年间，苏州的职业演员已达数千之众，每年苏州中秋夜的昆曲比赛，观众上千，热闹非凡。当时昆曲清唱是个全民运动，大概就像我们现在唱卡拉OK一样盛行，可见得中国人也是一个爱音乐爱唱歌的民族。由明万历到清乾嘉之间，昆曲独霸中国剧坛，足足兴盛了两百多年，其流传之广，历时之久，非其他剧种可望其项背。而又因为许多上层文人投入剧作，便将昆曲提升为"雅部"，成为雅俗共赏的一种精致艺术。明清的剧本作品数量惊人，其中名著如《牡丹亭》《长生殿》《桃花扇》早已成为文学经典。

（摘编自《我的昆曲之旅》，有删改）

生 词 New Words and Expressions

1.	雅俗共赏	yǎsú-gòngshǎng	appealing to both refined and popular tastes
2.	成书	chéngshū	be written
3.	鼎盛	dǐngshèng	at the height of prosperity
4.	王卿贵族	wángqīng guìzú	aristocrats
5.	市井小民	shìjǐng xiǎomín	plebeians
6.	举国若狂	jǔguó ruòkuáng	nationwide craze
7.	职业演员	zhíyè yǎnyuán	professional actor
8.	观众	guānzhòng	spectator, audience
9.	热闹非凡	rènao fēifán	extraordinarily bustling
10.	卡拉OK	kǎlā OK	karaoke
11.	盛行	shèngxíng	prevail
12.	音乐	yīnyuè	music
13.	独霸	dúbà	dominate
14.	剧坛	jùtán	the operatic world
15.	流传	liúchuán	spread
16.	历时	lìshí	last; take (a period of time)
17.	望其项背	wàngqí xiàngbèi	capable of catching up with sb
18.	剧本	jùběn	play script
19.	惊人	jīngrén	astonishing
20.	名著	míngzhù	masterpiece
21.	文学经典	wénxué jīngdiǎn	literature classic

文化词语

Cultural Words

1.	昆曲	kūnqǔ	*kunqu*, opera using kunqiang melodies and popular in southern Jiangsu Province, Beijing, and Hebei Province
2.	曹雪芹	Cáo Xuěqín	Cao Xueqin (1715–1763), author of *The Dream of the Red Chamber*

3.	《红楼梦》	"Hónglóu Mèng"	*The Dream of the Red Chamber*
4.	乾隆（年号）	Qiánlóng (niánhào)	1736–1795, Qing Dynasty reign title
5.	万历（年号）	Wànlì (niánhào)	1573–1620, Ming Dynasty reign title
6.	昆曲清唱	kūnqǔ qīngchàng	the activity of singing *kunqu* without instrumental accompaniment
7.	乾嘉（年号）	QiánJiā (niánhào)	1736–1820, Qing Dynasty reign titles (Qianlong and Jiaqing)
8.	雅部	yǎ bù	the refined opera, an other name for *kunqu*
9.	《牡丹亭》	"Mǔdān Tíng"	*The Peony Pavilion*
10.	《长生殿》	"Chángshēng Diàn"	*The Palace of Eternal Youth*
11.	《桃花扇》	"Táohuā Shàn"	*The Peach Blossom Fan*

课文理解练习 Text Comprehension

💡 **根据课文选一选** Choose the Right Answers Based on the Text

1. 明清两代的昆曲中心位于哪里？

苏州

杭州

广州

贵阳

2. 由明万历到清乾嘉之间，昆曲独霸中国剧坛，兴盛了多少年？

A 100 多年　　B 200 多年　　C 300 多年　　D 400 多年

💬 **根据提示说一说** Complete the Sentences Based on the Given Clues

1. 曹雪芹的《红楼梦》成书于乾隆年间，**正是昆曲鼎盛**之时。

（正）是……之时

1 每年苏州的中秋夜，＿＿＿＿＿＿＿＿。（开展昆曲比赛）

2 明清时期，＿＿＿＿＿＿＿＿。（全民热爱昆曲）

3 春节＿＿＿＿＿＿＿＿。（举家团圆）

4 清明节＿＿＿＿＿＿＿＿。（踏青扫墓）

2. 昆曲独霸中国剧坛，足足兴盛了两百年，其流传之广，历时之久，**非**其他剧种**可望其项背**。

非……可望其项背

1 景德镇的瓷器，历史悠久，做工精美，＿＿＿＿＿＿＿＿。（其他瓷器）

2 黄山景色秀美，＿＿＿＿＿＿＿＿。（其他名山）

3 北京故宫，气势恢宏，＿＿＿＿＿＿＿＿。（其他景点）

4 苏州拙政园，设计独特，＿＿＿＿＿＿＿＿。（其他园林）

文化理解练习 Cultural Reading Comprehension

读一读，选一选 Read and Choose

1. 曹雪芹在清朝乾隆年间创作了《红楼梦》，这个时期正是昆曲鼎盛之时，全国上下对昆曲都有极大的热情，由南到北，举国若狂。

❓ 下面哪个场景会在当时出现？（多选）

A 贵族在戏楼看昆曲表演　　B 市民哼唱着昆曲走在路上

C 某地不允许昆曲表演　　D 众多观众参加昆曲比赛

2. 我是昆曲演员，我给大家介绍一下昆曲。昆曲，以前叫"昆山腔"或"昆腔"，现在被称为"昆剧"。昆曲是中国最古老、影响最广泛的剧种之一，有"百戏之祖"的美誉。

❓ 以下哪一个不是昆曲的别称？

A 昆剧　　B 昆腔　　C 唱书　　D 昆山腔

文化小词库 Cultural Word Bank

- 昆山腔　　kūnshānqiāng　　*kunshanqiang*, another name of *kunqu* opera
- 昆腔　　kūnqiāng　　*kunqiang*, another name of *kunqu* opera
- 百戏之祖　bǎi xì zhī zǔ　　the Origin of Chinese Operas

课堂文化交际 Cultural Communication

 小组活动　Group Activity

选词填空，完成对话。再两人一组练习对话。

▎对话一 Dialogue 1

明清　昆曲　雅俗共赏　二百多年　《长生殿》　《桃花扇》

 李晶，你知道《牡丹亭》吗？

 《牡丹亭》是有名的 _____ 曲目，创作于明代。_____、_____ 也是非常知名的曲目。

 今天我听说昆曲在 _____ 两代，独霸剧坛，足足兴盛了 _____ 呢！

是啊！那时候，许多上层文人也创作剧本，将昆曲提升为"雅部"，使昆曲成为一种 _____ 的精致艺术。

对话二 Dialogue 2

苏州　乾隆　中秋　卡拉OK

有朋，昆曲的鼎盛时期是什么时候？

_____ 年间，是昆曲的鼎盛时期。

昆曲在哪个地区最流行呢？

明清两代，_____ 都是昆曲发展的中心，每年的 _____ 节，_____ 都举办昆曲比赛，特别热闹！

你的意思是昆曲在明清时期是全民行动，就像咱们现在唱 _____ 一样？

是的，大龙，你的比喻非常恰当！

课后文化实践 Cultural Practice

 个人活动 Individual Activity

请你查找资料了解《牡丹亭》的主人公是谁，讲了一个什么样的故事。下次课给大家介绍一下。

| 《牡丹亭》 | 主人公 | 故事情节 |

文化常识 **Cultural Knowledge**

昆曲 *Kunqu*

　　昆曲，原名"昆山腔"或简称"昆腔"，是中国古老的戏曲声腔、剧种，现被称为"昆剧"。昆曲是中国传统戏曲中最古老的剧种之一，是戏曲艺术中的瑰宝。昆曲发源于 14 世纪中国的苏州昆山，后经改良而走向全国，独领中国剧坛 200 多年。昆曲糅合了唱念做打、舞蹈及武术等艺术形式，以曲词典雅、行腔婉转、表演细腻著称，是被誉为"百戏之祖"的南戏系统之下的一个曲种。昆曲以鼓、板控制演唱节奏，以笛、三弦等为主要伴奏乐器，其唱念语音为"中州韵"。昆曲在 2001 年被联合国教科文组织列入"人类非物质文化遗产代表作名录"。

Kunqu, originally known as *kunshanqiang* (Kunshan tune), *kunqiang* (Kun tune) and more recently as *kunju* (Kun drama), is one of the oldest traditional operas of China. This much cherished operatic form is regarded as a treasure of Chinese traditional culture and art. Originated in Kunshan, Suzhou in the 14th century, *kunqu* was further refined before spreading nationwide. For over 200 years that followed, *kunqu* was the dominant opera on stage. *Kunqu* combines various art forms including singing, reciting, dramatic actions, dancing and martial arts, and is renown for its elegant and poetic lines, soft and graceful singing, and fine-grained performance. *Kunqu* is a type of Nanxi (South Dramas), a drama system reputed as the Origin of Chinese Operas. *Kunqu* music often employs drums and wooden clappers to control the beat, while bamboo flutes and sanxian (a three-stringed instrument) are the main accompanying instruments. This great cultural art is listed as the *Representative List of Intangible Cultural Heritage of Humanity* by UNESCO in 2001.

《牡丹亭》 *The Peony Pavilion*

《牡丹亭》是明代剧作家汤显祖的代表作，也是"古典四大名剧"之一。剧情主要内容是：官家千金杜丽娘与书生柳梦梅倾心相爱，后来杜丽娘因伤情而死，化为魂魄找到柳梦梅，他们人鬼相恋。最后杜丽娘起死回生，与柳梦梅永结同心。该剧描写了美好的爱情故事，体现了青年男女对自由爱情生活的追求。明代以来，《牡丹亭》一直是昆曲的经典剧目之一。

The Peony Pavilion is a representative work of the Ming Dynasty playwright Tang Xianzu. It is one of "the Four Great Classic Dramas". The main content of the plot is: Official's daughter Du Liniang and Scholar Liu Mengmei fell in love with each other. Later, due to lovesickness Du Liniang passed away but turned into a spirit to look for Liu Mengmei. Du Liniang found Liu Mengmei and they started their human-ghost romance. In the end, Du Liniang resurrected and became united with Liu Mengmei forever. It depicts the beautiful love story and portrays young people's pursuit of romantic freedom. From the Ming Dynasty onwards, *The Peony Pavilion* has been a repertoire of *kunqu*.

Zhōngguó　　piyǐngxì
中国皮影戏

课文 Text

　　皮影戏是中国民间戏剧的一种，表演时一般由三到五个艺人在白色幕布后面，用灯光照射兽皮或纸板做成的人物，形成剪影。一边操纵戏曲人物，一边唱述故事，同时配以打击乐器和弦乐。

　　两千多年前，汉武帝的爱妃生病去世，汉武帝思念心切，神情恍惚，不理朝政。术士李少翁有一天看到小孩子们手拿布娃娃玩耍，影子倒映在地上，栩栩如生。他就用布帛裁成李夫人的影像，涂上色彩，当夜晚来临时，用布遮挡成一个方形的空间，点上蜡烛，于是白布上出现了生动的剪影。汉武帝看后非常高兴。这个载入《汉书》的爱情故事被认为是皮影戏的渊源。

　　皮影戏在宋代已十分盛行；公元 13 世纪，传到了西亚；18 世纪传到了欧洲。据记载，1767 年，法国传教士把中国皮影戏带回法国，在巴黎演出，被称为"中国灯影"，轰动一时。后经法国人改造，成为"法兰西灯影"。中国的皮影戏对丰富世界艺坛做出了独特的贡献。华州皮影戏是中国乃至世界上最古老的艺术品种之一，被誉为"中华戏曲之父"和"世界电影之父"。

（摘编自《中国皮影戏》，有删改）

生词 New Words and Expressions

1.	灯光	dēngguāng	light
2.	照射	zhàoshè	light up
3.	兽皮	shòupí	leather
4.	纸板	zhǐbǎn	cardboard
5.	剪影	jiǎnyǐng	silhouette
6.	民间	mínjiān	folk
7.	幕布	mùbù	curtain
8.	操纵	cāozòng	control
9.	唱述	chàngshù	tell a story by singing
10.	打击乐器	dǎjī yuèqì	percussion instruments
11.	弦乐	xiányuè	string instruments
12.	生病	shēngbìng	get sick
13.	去世	qùshì	pass away
14.	思念心切	sīniàn xīnqiè	painfully miss someone
15.	神情恍惚	shénqíng huǎnghū	in a trance
16.	布娃娃	bùwáwa	cloth doll
17.	玩耍	wánshuǎ	play, have fun

18.	影子	yǐngzi	shadow
19.	倒映	dàoyìng	reflect
20.	栩栩如生	xǔxǔ rú shēng	vivid
21.	布帛	bùbó	cloth and silk
22.	裁	cái	cut
23.	影像	yǐngxiàng	image
24.	涂	tú	colour, paint
25.	色彩	sècǎi	colour
26.	遮挡	zhēdǎng	cover
27.	蜡烛	làzhú	candle
28.	渊源	yuānyuán	origin
29.	欧洲	Ōuzhōu	Europe
30.	法国	Fǎguó	France
31.	传教士	chuánjiàoshì	missionary
32.	轰动一时	hōngdòng yìshí	create a great sensation
33.	改造	gǎizào	reform, remake
34.	艺坛	yìtán	the world of art
35.	乃至	nǎizhì	and even

文化词语
Cultural Words

1.	皮影戏	píyǐngxì	shadow puppetry
2.	汉武帝	Hàn Wǔdì	Emperor Wu of the Han Dynasty
3.	爱妃	àifēi	beloved concubine

4. 朝政	cháozhèng	state affairs
5. 术士	shùshì	alchemist
6.《汉书》	"Hàn Shū"	*History of the Han Dynasty*, a dynastic history by Ban Gu (32–92)
7. 华州	Huàzhōu	Huazhou District in Shaanxi Province

课文理解练习 Text Comprehension

 根据课文选一选 Choose the Right Answers Based on the Text

1. 皮影戏是一种用灯光照射什么而形成剪影的民间戏剧？

A 兽皮或木板　　B 纸板或木板　　C 兽皮或纸板　　D 布或丝绸

2. 汉武帝和他的爱妃的爱情故事被认为是皮影戏的渊源，它曾被载入哪部作品？

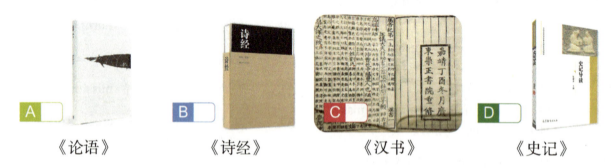

A《论语》　　　　B《诗经》　　　　C《汉书》　　　　D《史记》

根据提示说一说 Complete the Sentences Based on the Given Clues

1. 表演时，一般由三到五个艺人在白色幕布后面，一边操纵戏曲人物，一边唱述故事。

一边……，一边……

❶ 大龙：为什么说京剧是视听结合的艺术？

有朋：因为看京剧时，要 ＿＿＿＿＿＿＿＿＿。（听唱腔、看身段）

❷ 大龙：王爷爷听戏的时候，为什么手也在跟着动？

有朋：戏迷喜欢 ＿＿＿＿＿＿＿＿＿。（听戏、打拍子）

③ 大龙：爬山太累了！

有朋：我们可以到亭子里 _____。（休息、观赏景色）

④ 大龙：你们除夕是怎么过的？

有朋：我们全家人聚在一起，_____。（看春晚、吃饺子）

2. 这个载入《汉书》的爱情故事<u>被认为</u>是皮影戏的渊源。

[名] + 被认为是 + [名]

① 华州皮影戏 _____。（中国乃至世界上最古老的艺术品种之一）

② 昆曲 _____。（中国最古老的剧种之一）

③ 昆曲的发源地 _____。（苏州的昆山）

④ 京剧 _____。（中国的国粹）

文化理解练习 Cultural Reading Comprehension

 读一读，选一选 Read and Choose

1. 我是伊人，今天我跟着一位皮影表演艺人，参观了皮影的制作过程。首先要挑选材料，皮影的材料主要为牛皮或驴皮。第二步是制皮，将选好的皮放入清水中泡着，然后用刀刮制。第三步是画稿，设计出不同的人物。之后依次还有过稿、雕刻、上色等几个复杂的步骤。

❓ 制作皮影的第四个步骤是什么？

A 制皮　　B 画稿　　C 过稿　　D 上色

小词库 Word Bank

- 驴皮　lǘpí　donkey skin
- 刮制　guāzhì　scrape
- 画稿　huàgǎo　a step in shadow puppet production where one draws patterns on dried animal skin
- 过稿　guògǎo　a step in shadow puppet production where one sews the patterns previously drawn onto dried animal skin with thread
- 上色　shàngsè　colouring

2. 我是一名皮影戏的表演艺人，我每次表演的时候都很忙碌。我一边用几根竹棍控制皮影人物，一边唱述故事，脚下还要控制锣鼓。演皮影的屏幕，是用一块1平方米大小的白布做成的。演出的时候，我配合着音乐声舞动人物，让皮影紧贴着屏幕活动。观众看表演时常常会鼓掌欢呼。

❓ 以下哪一个选项不会出现在皮影戏的表演现场?

A 用竹棍来控制人物

B 用锣鼓来制造音乐

C 把纸板当作演皮影的屏幕

D 表演艺人唱述故事

小词库 Word Bank		
• 忙碌	mánglù	busy
• 竹棍	zhúgùn	bamboo stick
• 屏幕	píngmù	screen
• 白布	báibù	white gauze
• 鼓掌	gǔzhǎng	clap one's hands, applause
• 欢呼	huānhū	exclaim

课堂文化交际 Cultural Communication

 小组活动 Group Activity

选词填空，完成对话。再两人一组练习对话。

┃ 对话一 Dialogue 1

色彩　流传　两千多　剪影　渊源　蜡烛

 李晶，你知道皮影戏的起源吗?

 皮影戏最早出现在 ＿＿＿＿＿＿ 年前，关于它的起源 ＿＿＿＿＿＿ 着一个美丽的爱情故事。

 是什么爱情故事呢?

据说，汉武帝的爱妃死后，术士用布帛做成她的影像，涂上 _____。到了晚上，他用布挡成一个方形的空间，点上 _____ 之后，白布上就出现了生动的 _____，汉武帝看后非常高兴。

好浪漫的故事，所以这个故事可以看作是皮影戏的 _____，对吗？

是的，伊人，你说得很对！

对话二 Dialogue 2

古老　法兰西灯影　华州皮影戏　世界电影之父

有朋，你知道皮影戏为什么又叫"中国灯影"吗？

1767 年，法国传教士把中国皮影戏带到巴黎演出，轰动一时，于是有了这个说法。后经法国人改造，成为 _____。

我听说 _____ 是中国乃至世界上最 _____ 的艺术品种之一。

是的，_____ 被誉为"中华戏曲之父"和"_____"。

课后文化实践 Cultural Practice

个人活动 Individual Activity

请查找资料，观赏一段中国皮影戏，了解关于皮影的起源、种类、做法和地位等，下次课给大家介绍一下。

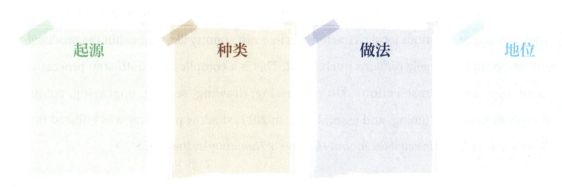

起源　　　种类　　　做法　　　地位

皮影戏 Shadow Puppetry

皮影戏又称"影戏"或"灯影戏"，是中国民间古老的传统艺术，一种以兽皮或纸板做成的人物剪影以表演故事的民间戏剧。表演时，艺人们在白色幕布后面，一边操纵皮影，一边唱述故事，同时配以打击乐器和弦乐，有浓厚的乡土气息。据记载，皮影戏在元代传至西亚，几百年后传至欧洲，可谓历史悠久，源远流长。中国地域广阔，各地的皮影都有自己的特色，其制作程序大多相似，通常要经过选皮、制皮、画稿、过稿、镂刻、敷彩、发汗熨平、缀结合成等多道工序。2011 年，中国皮影戏入选联合国教科文组织"人类非物质文化遗产代表作名录"。

Shadow puppetry, alternatively known as "shadow play" and "shadow puppet", is an ancient folk art in China. It is a folk story-telling performance which utilises human sculptures cut out from leather or cardboard. During a shadow puppetry, puppeteers hide behind a white screen and control puppets while singing stories in local tunes. Percussion and string instruments further add a rich country flavour to the show. According to historical documents, shadow puppetry boasts a long history. During the Yuan Dynasty, shadow puppetry spread to Western Asia, and several hundred years later, it also reached Europe. It is imaginable that shadow puppetry gradually acquired various local characteristics in a vast country like China, but the production of shadow puppetry largely remains unchanged. This is a complicated multi-step process which involves animal skin selection, skin processing, drawing, sewing, engraving, colouring, dehydrating and flattening, and assembling. In 2011, shadow puppetry was enlisted into *the Representative List of Intangible Cultural Heritage of Humanity* by the UNESCO.

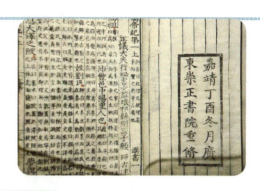

《汉书》 *History of the Han Dynasty*

　　《汉书》是中国第一部纪传体断代史，"二十四史"之一，由东汉史学家班固编撰，是继《史记》之后中国古代又一部重要史书，与《史记》《后汉书》《三国志》并称为"前四史"。《汉书》全书主要记述了自西汉的汉高祖元年（公元前 206 年）至新朝王莽地皇四年（公元 23 年）共 230 年的史事。《汉书》包括纪十二篇，表八篇，志十篇，传七十篇，共一百篇，后人划分为一百二十卷，共八十万字。《汉书》这种纪传体的断代史体裁，是班固首先创造的。以后中国历代的"正史"都采用了这种体裁。

　　History of the Han Dynasty, is the first biographical dynastic history of China compiled by historian Ban Gu of the Eastern Han Dynasty. Reputed as one of the "Twenty-Four Histories", *History of the Han Dynasty* is another significant history book in ancient China after the *Records of the Grand Historian*. The two aforementioned books are among the so-called "Four Early Histories", together with *The History of the Eastern Han Dynasty* and *Records of the Three Kingdoms*. Spanning a timeline of 230 years, *History of the Han Dynasty* mainly recounts the history from the first year of Emperor Han Gaozu's reign in the Western Han Dynasty (206 BC) to the fourth year of the Dihuang Emperor Wang Mang's reign in the Xin (New) Dynasty (23 AD). Totaling 800,000 words, the book consists of 100 sections (later categorized into 120 volumes), which include 12 Ji (Imperial Biographies), 8 Biao (Event Records), 10 Zhi (Records of Institutional Reforms), and 70 Zhuan (Biographies). *History of the Han Dynasty* was a dynastic history specifically dedicated to the Western Han Dynasty. This form of history writing is an important creation and significant contribution of the author Ban Gu, and all official histories of subsequent dynasties followed this form.

单元自评
Self-Assessment

本单元我们学习了有关中国"戏曲文化"的中文表达和文化知识。请你用下面的表格检查一下自己的学习成果吧！如果 5 个中国结是满分，你会给自己几个呢？In this unit, we have learned expressions and cultural knowledge about *Culture in Chinese Opera*. Please make use of the table below to evaluate your learning. If five Chinese knots mean full completion, how many will you give yourself?

第 13 课		🔴	🔴🔴	🔴🔴🔴	🔴🔴🔴🔴	🔴🔴🔴🔴🔴
🏮 我会使用下列句型。	·把 +（什么）+ 称为 +（什么）					
	·……象征着……					
🏮 我知道下列中国文化知识。	·京剧					
	·梅兰芳					
🏮 我能为我的朋友介绍京剧。						
第 14 课		🔴	🔴🔴	🔴🔴🔴	🔴🔴🔴🔴	🔴🔴🔴🔴🔴
🏮 我会使用下列句型。	·（正）是……之时					
	·非……可望其项背					
🏮 我知道下列中国文化知识。	·昆曲					
	·《牡丹亭》					
🏮 我能为我的朋友介绍《牡丹亭》。						
第 15 课		🔴	🔴🔴	🔴🔴🔴	🔴🔴🔴🔴	🔴🔴🔴🔴🔴
🏮 我会使用下列句型。	·一边……，一边……					
	·[名] + 被认为是 + [名]					
🏮 我知道下列中国文化知识。	·皮影戏					
	·《汉书》					
🏮 我能为我的朋友介绍皮影戏。						

扩展 Further Extension

🏮 关于中国"戏曲文化"，我还了解了以下内容：

1. _____

2. _____

第六单元
UNIT ❻

中国智慧
Chinese Wisdom

16

第16课
Lesson 16

Zhèng xiàng què yú
郑相 却鱼

课 文 Text

从前，有人赠送鱼给郑国的宰相，郑国的宰相没有接受。有人问郑国的宰相："你平时爱吃鱼，为什么不接受别人赠送的鱼呢？"郑国的宰相回答说："我爱吃鱼，因此不能接受鱼。如果接受别人赠  送的鱼会让我失去官职，没有俸禄，以后就无鱼可吃了；如果我不接受，清廉为官，就可以保住我的官职，我一辈子都可以吃鱼。"

原文

昔者有馈鱼于郑相者，郑相不受。或谓郑相曰："子嗜鱼，何故不受？"对曰："吾以嗜鱼，故不受鱼。受鱼失禄，无以食鱼；不受得禄，终身食鱼。"

选自《新序·节士》

生 词 New Words and Expressions

1.	从前	cóngqián	in the past		5.	官职	guānzhí	official position
2.	赠送	zèngsòng	give		6.	俸禄	fènglù	salary
3.	接受	jiēshòu	accept		7.	保住	bǎozhù	keep
4.	失去	shīqù	lose		8.	一辈子	yíbèizi	all one's life, a life

文化词语
Cultural Words

1. 郑相却鱼　　Zhèng xiàng què yú　the Premier of Zheng refuses the gift of fish
2. 郑国　　　　Zhèngguó　　　　　Zheng state
3. 宰相　　　　zǎixiàng　　　　　premiere, chancellor
4. 清廉为官　　qīnglián wéiguān　work as a government official free of corruption

课文理解练习 Text Comprehension

根据课文选一选 Choose the Right Answers Based on the Text

1. 郑国的宰相为什么没有接受别人送他的鱼？

　　A 因为他不爱吃鱼　　　B 因为他觉得别人送他的鱼不新鲜了

　　C 因为他想清廉为官　　D 因为他现在不想吃鱼

2. 宰相的做法没有体现出下列的哪一种思想？

　　A 深谋远虑　　　B 清正廉洁

　　C 心存敬畏　　　D 以权谋私

根据提示说一说 Complete the Sentences Based on the Given Clues

1. 我爱吃鱼，因此不接受鱼。 ……，因此……

❶ 我如果失去官职就无鱼可吃，＿＿＿＿＿＿＿＿＿。（不接受）

❷ 颐和园里有座长桥，共有 17 个桥洞，＿＿＿＿＿＿＿＿。（十七孔桥）

❸ 各国的文化和习俗不同，＿＿＿＿＿＿＿＿＿。（互相理解、尊重）

❹ 昆明气候宜人，四季如春，＿＿＿＿＿＿＿＿。（春城）

2. 如果接受别人赠送的鱼会让我失去官职，没有俸禄，以后就无鱼可吃了。 无+[名]+可+[动]

❶ 故宫里的一些猫是＿＿＿＿＿＿＿的流浪猫。（家、归）

❷ 没赶上高铁，我非常着急，却又＿＿＿＿＿＿＿。（计、施）

❸ 亭子的前面已经＿＿＿＿＿＿＿，只能原路返回。（路、走）

❹ 登上长城那一刻，我沉默了，不是因为我＿＿＿＿＿＿＿，而是我还没想好如何形容我的激动之情。（话、说）

文化理解练习 Cultural Reading Comprehension

 **读一读，选一选** Read and Choose

中国有句俗语：授人以鱼不如授人以渔。授人以鱼，只供一饭之需；授人以渔，终生受用无穷。

1. "渔"是什么意思？

Ⓐ "渔"同"鱼"　　Ⓑ 钓鱼的工具　　Ⓒ 鱼筐　　Ⓓ 捕鱼的方法

2. "授人以鱼不如授人以渔"的意思是？

　A　吃一条鱼吃不饱，吃很多条鱼才能吃饱。

　B　送鱼不礼貌，因为我们不知道别人是否爱吃鱼。

　C　如果想让人永远都有鱼吃，那应该教给他捕鱼的方法。

　D　给别人鱼不如约他一起钓鱼。

文化小词库 Cultural Word Bank

- 授人以鱼不如授人以渔　shòu rén yǐ yú bùrú shòu rén yǐ yú
  Give a man a fish and you feed him for a day; teach a man to fish and you feed him for a lifetime.

课堂文化交际 Cultural Communication

小组活动　Group Activity

两人一组编对话，比比哪组更精彩。

要求：一个人的观点是要把握眼前的机会，机不可失，失不再来；另一个人的观点是不应该只看眼前利益，而是应该有长远的眼光。

二鸟在林，不如一鸟在手　人无远虑，必有近忧　珍惜　享受　当下
远见　未来

课后文化实践 Cultural Practice

个人活动　Individual Activity

请查资料找一找其他体现不拘泥于眼前利益，而是具有长远眼光的成语或者故事，下次课跟同学们分享一下。

陶母退鱼 Tao's Mother Returned the Fish

陶母退鱼的典故，又叫"陶母封鲊"，是《世说新语·贤媛第十九》中记载的一个故事。陶侃青年时是一名管理河道及渔业的官吏，曾经派官府里的差役把一坛腌鱼送给他的母亲。陶侃的母亲将送来的腌鱼封好交还给差役，还写了一封回信责备陶侃，信中写到：你身为官吏本应清正廉洁，却用官府的东西作为礼品赠送给我，这样做不仅没有好处，反而增加我的忧愁。

The story of "Tao's mother returned the fish" is recorded in Chapter 19 "Xianyuan (Worthy Beauties)" of *Shishuo Xinyu · A New Account of Tales of the World*. The story goes that, when he was young, Tao Kan worked as a government official in charge of managing river canals and fishing. He once sent an employee on an errand home, taking a jar of preserved fish to his mother. Tao Kan's mother sealed the fish jar and asked the employee to take it back. She also wrote Tao Kan a letter, in which she reproached her son, "As a government official, you should be free of all corruption. But now you have given me some public property as a gift. Doing so by no means benefits me, but only adds to my woe."

临渊羡鱼，不如退而结网 It's Better to Withdraw and Make a Net than to Stand by the Pond and Long for Fish

此句出自《淮南子·说林训》，原文是：临河而羡鱼，不如归家织网。意思是站在水边想得到鱼，不如回家去结网。这个典故阐明的是愿望与行动之间的关系，比喻只有愿望而没有行动，

对事情毫无好处，或者比喻只希望得到而不将希望付诸行动。正如我们的目的是打鱼，但只有"退"而织好网，才有可能得到鱼。

Recorded in the chapter "*Shuo Lin Xun*" of *Huai Nan Zi*, this idiom conveys the message that dreaming without action is no good for the realisation of dreams. This expression illustrates the inner logic between aim and action. For instance, the aim of obtaining fish is only a dream without "withdrawing" and weaving a net.

17

第 **17** 课
Lesson 17

Zēngzǐ　shǒuxìn
曾子守信

课文 Text

曾子的妻子要到集市去，她的儿子跟在她后面边走边哭。曾子的妻子对儿子说："你先回家，等我回来后杀猪给你吃。"妻子从集市回来后，曾子就抓了一只猪准备杀了它，妻子连忙制止他说："刚才我只不过是跟小孩子闹着玩儿的罢了。"曾子说："小孩子是不能和他闹着玩儿的。小孩子不懂事，要依靠父母而逐步学习，听从父母的教诲。现在你欺骗他，是教他学会欺骗。要是母亲欺骗儿子，儿子就不会再相信自己的母亲了，这不是正确教育孩子该用的方法。"于是曾子就杀猪、煮猪给孩子吃了。

原文

曾子之妻之市，其子随之而泣。其母曰："汝还。顾反为汝杀彘。"妻适市来，曾子欲捕彘杀之。妻止之曰："特与婴儿戏耳。"曾子曰："婴儿非与戏耳。婴儿非有知也，待父母而学者也，听父母之教。今子欺之是教子欺也。母欺子，子而不信其母，非所以成教也。"遂烹彘也。

选自《韩非子·外储说左上》

生词 New Words and Expressions

1.	集市	jíshì	marketplace
2.	杀	shā	kill
3.	猪	zhū	pig
4.	抓	zhuā	catch
5.	准备	zhǔnbèi	prepare
6.	制止	zhìzhǐ	stop
7.	闹着玩儿	nàozhe wánr	say or do something as a joke

8.	罢了	bà le	merely
9.	懂事	dǒngshì	intelligent
10.	逐步	zhúbù	gradually
11.	教诲	jiàohuì	teaching
12.	欺骗	qīpiàn	deceive
13.	正确	zhèngquè	correct
14.	教育	jiàoyù	educate
15.	煮	zhǔ	boil

文化词语
Cultural Words

1. 曾子　　Zēngzǐ　　Zengzi (505 BC–436 BC), Chinese philosopher

课文理解练习 Text Comprehension

根据课文选一选 Choose the Right Answers Based on the Text

1. 曾子的妻子为什么答应孩子杀猪?

A 因为她想吃猪肉　　　　　　B 因为孩子想吃猪肉

C 因为她想让孩子回家而找了一个借口　　D 因为她想吓唬孩子

2. 文中的曾子是怎样的形象?

A 慷慨大方　　B 见义勇为　　C 出尔反尔　　D 诚实守信

根据提示说一说 Complete the Sentences Based on the Given Clues

1. 你先回家，等我回来后杀猪给你吃。 ……给+[名/代]+[动]……

① 母亲节快到了，我 _____ 一支口红。（买）

② 今天我做一道宫保鸡丁 _____。（吃）

③ 请有朋写副春联 _____。（欣赏）

④ 请伊人唱一段京剧 _____。（听）

2. 现在你欺骗他，是教他学会欺骗。 ……教+[名/代]+[动]……

① 中国人吃饭的时候习惯用筷子，大龙刚来中国的时候，有朋 _____。（用筷子）

② 如果外国朋友去中国人家里过新年，中国人会 _____。（包饺子）

③ 大龙想学习中国书法，有朋先 _____。（握笔）

④ 我和奶奶去超市购物，我 _____。（扫码支付）

文化理解练习 Cultural Reading Comprehension

 **读一读，选一选** Read and Choose

　　我叫季布，生活在汉初。只要是我答应过的事情，无论有多大的困难，我都会设法办到，受到大家的赞扬，世上流传着这样的谚语："得黄金百斤，不如得季布一诺"，这是成语"一诺千金"的由来。后来，我得罪了汉高祖刘邦，被悬赏捉拿，我的朋友不被重金所诱惑，冒险保护我，使我免遭祸殃。

1. 和"一诺千金"意思不同的成语是？

Ⓐ 说一不二　　Ⓑ 说三道四　　Ⓒ 言而有信　　Ⓓ 季布一诺

2. 季布免遭祸殃的原因是什么？

A 季布非常聪明，找到了逃跑的办法。   B 季布的地位很高。

C 季布言而有信，因此他得到了朋友的帮助。   D 季布没有遇到困难。

小词库 Word Bank

- 赞扬　　zànyáng
  praise
- 悬赏捉拿　xuánshǎng zhuōná
  offer a reward for the capture of someone
- 诱惑　　yòuhuò
  tempt
- 保护　　bǎohù
  protect
- 免遭祸殃　miǎnzāo huòyāng
  spare someone calamity

文化小词库 Cultural Word Bank

- 一诺千金　　yínuò qiānjīn
  A promise is worth a thousand *liang* of gold.
- 刘邦　　Liú Bāng
  Liu Bang (256 BC–195 BC), founder and first emperor of the Han Dynasty

课堂文化交际 Cultural Communication

 小组活动 Group Activity

每个人给大家讲一个关于守时或者守信的小故事，看看谁的故事最精彩。

课后文化实践 Cultural Practice

 个人活动 Individual Activity

请你上网查一查还有哪些关于守时守信的成语，下次课给大家说一说。

曾子 Zengzi

曾子（前 505 年—前 436 年），原名曾参（shēn），字子舆，鲁国南武城（今山东费县）人。春秋末年思想家，孔门弟子七十二贤之一，儒家学派的重要代表人物。曾子秉承了儒家"以仁为尊的伦理观，倡导"明仁道，通忠恕，重修身，守孝心，不苟权贵"的君子品格。曾子主持了《论语》的编写，并撰写了《礼记·大学》等儒家典籍。曾子在儒学发展史上占有重要的地位，后世尊其为"宗圣"。

Zengzi (505 BC–436 BC), also known as Zeng Shen, style name Ziyu, was born in Nanwu City, Lu State (today's Feixian of Shandong Province). He was a philosopher in the late Spring and Autumn Period, one of 72 virtuous disciples of Confucius, and a renowned representative of Confucianism. Zengzi adhered to the Confucian ethical concept of "benevolence", and advocated the gentlemanly character of "valuing benevolence, loyalty and forgiveness, the cultivation of one's moral character, filial piety, and not giving in to power and nobility". Zengzi was involved in the compiling of *The Analects of Confucius* and authored various works such as *The Great Learning*. For his significance throughout the development of Confucianism, Zengzi is revered as "Zongsheng (The Ancestral Sage)".

曾子避席 Zengzi Walked Away from the Mat

"曾子避席"出自《孝经》。一次，曾子在孔子身边侍坐，孔子问他："以前的圣贤之王有至高无上的德行和精要奥妙的理论，用来教导天下之人，人们能和睦相处，君王和臣下之间也没有不满。你知道是什么吗？"曾子听了，明白老师孔子是要指点他最深刻的道理，于是立刻从坐着的席子上站起来，走到席子外面，恭恭敬敬地回答："我不够聪明，哪里能知道，还请老师把这些道理教给我。"在这里，"避席"是一种非常礼貌的行为，当曾子听到老师要向他传授道理时，他站起身来，走到席子外向老师请教，是为了表示他对老师的尊重，后世常用"避席"表示学生对老师的尊敬。

"Zengzi walked away from the mat" is a famed story recorded in *The Classic of Filial Piety*. One day, Zengzi was sitting next to his teacher Confucius, who asked him, "The sage kings of the past guided all under heaven with utmost morality and profound theories, so that people lived in harmony and disaffection was nonexistent between rulers and their courtiers. Do you know how they did it?" Upon hearing this, Zengzi understood that Confucius was going to teach him the most profound knowledge. He rose from the mat, walked away and said in a humble voice, "I do not have enough intelligence to comprehend this, and I sincerely wish that you could enlighten me." Here, the act of walking away from the mat is a gesture of respect. When Zengzi knew that Confucius was about to teach him something of significance, he stood up and walked away, consulting his teacher from outside the mat. It is often used to indicate students' respect to the teacher.

18

第18课
Lesson 18

Zǐgòng shú rén yǔ
子贡赎人与
Zǐlù zhěng nì
子路拯溺

热身活动 Warm Up

1. 请说说中文里有哪些与守时守信相关的成语。
2. 你觉得你会见义勇为吗? 做了好事之后, 你会接受别人的回报吗?

课文 Text

　　鲁国有一条法律, 鲁国人在其他诸侯国沦为奴隶时, 如果有人把他们赎出来, 那么这个人就可以从国家获得补偿金。有一次, 孔子的学生子贡把一个鲁国人赎了回来, 但他没有向国家领取补偿金。孔子说:"子贡做错了! 你向国家领取补偿金, 不会损伤你的品行; 可是你不领取补偿金, 鲁国就没有人再去赎回自己受困的同胞了。"

　　子路救起一名溺水者, 那人为了表示感谢, 送了他一头牛, 子路收下了。孔子高兴地说:"鲁国人从此一定会勇于救落水者了。"孔子见微知著, 洞察人情, 实在是了不起。

原文

　　鲁国之法, 鲁人为人臣妾于诸侯, 有能赎之者, 取其金于府。子贡赎鲁人于诸侯, 来而让, 不取其金。孔子曰:"赐失之矣。自今以往, 鲁人不赎人矣。取其金则无损于行, 不取其金则不复赎人矣。"

　　子路拯溺者, 其人拜之以牛, 子路受之。孔子曰:"鲁人必多拯溺者矣。"孔子见之以细, 观化远也。

选自《吕氏春秋·先识览·察微》

生词 New Words and Expressions

1.	法律	fǎlǜ	law
2.	沦为	lúnwéi	be reduced to
3.	奴隶	núlì	slave
4.	赎	shú	ransom
5.	获得	huòdé	acquire, receive
6.	补偿金	bǔcháng jīn	compensation
7.	领取	lǐngqǔ	receive
8.	损伤	sǔnshāng	harm
9.	品行	pǐnxíng	moral conduct
10.	受困	shòukùn	be trapped
11.	同胞	tóngbāo	compatriot
12.	救	jiù	save
13.	溺水者	nìshuǐzhě	drowning person
14.	感谢	gǎnxiè	thank
15.	勇于	yǒngyú	be brave to
16.	落水者	luòshuǐ zhě	drowning person
17.	见微知著	jiànwēi zhīzhù	recognise the whole through observation of a small part
18.	洞察	dòngchá	perceive
19.	人情	rénqíng	human emotions
20.	实在	shízài	truly, virtually

文化词语
Cultural Words

1. 鲁国　Lǔ Guó　State of Lu, one of the Warring States into which China was divided during the Eastern Zhou Period (770 BC–256 BC)
2. 子贡　Zǐgòng　Zigong, student of Confucius
3. 子路　Zǐlù　Zilu, student of Confucius

课文理解练习 Text Comprehension

 根据课文选一选 Choose the Right Answers Based on the Text

1. 孔子认为子贡应不应该领取赎金？

A 应该，这样鲁国人才会继续赎回受难的同胞。

B 应该，这样鲁国人就不会继续赎回受难的同胞了。

C 不应该，这样鲁国人才会继续赎回受难的同胞。

D 不应该，这样鲁国人就不会继续赎回受难的同胞。

2. 子路为什么收下了那头牛？

A 因为他想吃牛肉。　　　　　　　 B 因为他想养牛。

C 因为他想倡导善有善报的社会规则。　 D 因为他害怕孔子责备他。

 根据提示说一说 Complete the Sentences Based on the Given Clues

1. 如果有人能把他们赎出来，就可以从国家获得补偿金。

……[动] + 出来……

1 五岳是哪几座山？你可以 ＿＿＿＿＿＿＿＿ 吗？（说）

2 穿着唐装的伊人，如同从古代画中 ＿＿＿＿＿＿＿＿ 的美女。（走）

3 冲一杯龙井茶，会有淡淡的茶香从杯中 ＿＿＿＿＿＿＿＿ 。（飘）

4 学中文一年多了，大龙可以 ＿＿＿＿＿＿＿＿ 好几首唐诗。（背）

2. 子路救起一名溺水者，那人为了表示感谢，送了他一头牛，子路收下了。

……[动] + [动/形]……

1 北京胡同的名字都起得十分别致，很容易就 ＿＿＿＿＿＿＿＿ 。（记住）

2 春节的时候，家家户户都 ＿＿＿＿＿＿＿＿ 春联。（贴上）

3 今天我们学习了"子贡赎人"的故事，老师讲了一遍，我就 ＿＿＿＿＿＿＿＿ 。（听懂）

4 元宵节的灯谜，只有大龙一个人 ＿＿＿＿＿＿＿＿ 。（猜到）

文化理解练习 Cultural Reading Comprehension

读一读，选一选 Read and Choose

 我是子贡，我姓端木，是孔子的学生。我曾经担任过鲁国、卫国的丞相。我还善于经商，是我们师门中的首富。"端木遗风"说的就是我遗留下来的诚信经商的风气。"君子爱财，取之有道"是我的经商理念，为后世商

界所推崇。

1. 下列哪个人不是孔子的学生？

   A 子贡　　B 子路　　C 曾子　　D 老子

2. "君子爱财，取之有道"的意思是？

   A 君子喜爱一切财物。

   B 君子不喜爱财物。

   C 君子喜欢正道得到的财物，不要不义之财。

   D 君子喜欢正道得到的财物，但是也要不义之财。

小词库 Word Bank

- 经商　jīngshāng
  business management
- 首富　shǒufù
  the richest person
- 推崇　tuīchóng
  promote

文化小词库 Cultural Word Bank

- 卫国　　　　　　　　Wèi Guó　　　　　　　　State of Wei
- 端木遗风　　　　　　Duānmù yífēng　　　　　the Duanmu (family name of Zigong) legacy
- 君子爱财，取之有道　jūnzǐ àicái, qǔzhī yǒudào　A gentlemen makes money in the right way.

课堂文化交际 Cultural Communication

小组活动　Group Activity

两人一组编对话，比比哪组更精彩。

一方的观点是：做好事应该接受回报；另一方的观点是：做好事不应该接受回报。

子贡赎人　子路拯溺　善有善报　做好事不留名

课后文化实践 Cultural Practice

孔子的名言

个人活动　Individual Activity

请你查找资料，了解孔子说过的名言，思考一下你认同哪些，不认同哪些？为什么？

孔门七十二贤 The Seventy-Two Virtuous Disciples of Confucius

中国古代著名的思想家和教育家孔子的七十二位圣贤弟子被称为孔门七十二贤。《史记·孔子世家》记载："孔子以诗、书、礼、乐教，弟子盖三千焉，身通六艺者七十有二人。""孔门七十二贤"是孔子思想和学说的坚定追随者和实践者，也是儒学的积极传播者。孔子对弟子因材施教，始于德行、言语，达于政事、文学，先后有阶序，德才兼备是孔子教育弟子成才的目标。

The Seventy-Two Virtuous Disciples of Confucius refer to the 72 virtuous disciples of the great thinker and educator Confucius. As recorded in "the Biography of Confucius" of the *Records of the Great Historian*, "Confucius lectured in poetry, classics, etiquette, and music to roughly 3000 disciples, of whom 72 were fully versed in the six arts." The Seventy-Two Virtuous Disciples of Confucianism were devoted followers and practitioners of Confucian thoughts and theories, and worked ardently to spread them to a wider audience. Confucius tailored his teaching to fit the different characteristics of his disciples. Learning is progressive in nature — it starts with the study of morality and eloquence, and peaks at government management and literature. To cultivate students with both morality and ability was the ultimate goal of Confucius.

子贡 Zigong

　　子贡（前520年—？），复姓端木，名赐，字子贡，春秋末年卫国（今河南省）人。他是孔子的得意门生之一，能言善辩，行事通达，也是社会活动家和杰出的外交家，曾任鲁国、卫国的丞相。子贡同时还是著名的富商，被尊称为"儒商"鼻祖。在《论语》中，子贡的名字多次出现。子贡在传播孔子的学说中发挥了重要作用，是孔子学说的主要"代言人"。司马迁《史记·仲尼弟子列传》对子贡所用笔墨最多，就篇幅而言在孔门众弟子中是最长的。

　　Zigong (520 BC-？), family name Duanmu, given name Ci, was born in the State of Wei (today's Henan Province) during the late Spring and Autumn Period. Being eloquent and versed in the ways of the world, Zigong was a favourite student of Confucius. He was a social activist and distinguished diplomat, and served as Premiere of States of Lu and Wei. Meanwhile, he was a much famed businessman and is known as the forefather of Confucian businessmen. Appearing many times in *The Analects of Confucius*, Zigong is practically a spokesperson for Confucianism, and it was through his efforts that the Confucian doctrines spread to the masses. In his *Records of the Grand Historian*, Sima Qian devoted the most energy and space to Zigong in "the Biographies of Confucius' Disciples".

单元自评
Self-Assessment

本单元我们学习了有关中国"中国智慧"的中文表达和文化知识。请你用下面的表格检查一下自己的学习成果吧！如果 5 个中国结是满分，你会给自己几个呢？ In this unit, we have learned expressions and cultural knowledge about Chinese Wisdom.Please make use of the table below to evaluate your learning. If five Chinese knots mean full completion, how many will you give yourself?

第 16 课		❀	❀❀	❀❀❀	❀❀❀❀	❀❀❀❀❀
🏮 我会使用下列句型。	•……，因此……					
	无+[名]+可+[动]					
🏮 我知道下列中国文化知识。	•陶母退鱼					
	•临渊羡鱼，不如退而结网					
🏮 我能理解"郑相却鱼"的含义。						
第 17 课		❀	❀❀	❀❀❀	❀❀❀❀	❀❀❀❀❀
🏮 我会使用下列句型。	•……给+[名/代]+[动]……					
	•……教+[名/代]+[动]……					
🏮 我知道下列中国文化知识。	•曾子					
	•曾子避席					
🏮 我能理解"一诺千金"的含义。						
第 18 课		❀	❀❀	❀❀❀	❀❀❀❀	❀❀❀❀❀
🏮 我会使用下列句型。	•……[动]+出来					
	•……[动]+[动/形]……					
🏮 我知道下列中国文化知识。	•孔门七十二贤					
	•子贡					
🏮 我能理解"子贡赎人"和"子路拯溺"的故事。						
扩展 Further Extension						

🏮 关于"中国智慧"，我还了解了以下内容：

1. _____

2. _____

附 录

◆ 文化短语

生词表 Vocabulary

生词	拼音	译文		生词	拼音	译文	
挨着个儿	āizhe gèr	one by one	1	按照	ànzhào	according to	4
◆ 爱妃	àifēi	beloved concubine	15	暗中	ànzhōng	on the sly	2

生词	拼音	译文		生词	拼音	译文	
◆ 八卦	bāguà	Eight Trigrams	11	保住	bǎozhù	keep	16
◆ 八旗子弟	bāqí zǐdì	children of the Eight Banners	11	◆ 北平	Běipíng	the old name of Beijing	11
把柄	bǎbǐng	handle	10	鼻梁	bíliáng	nose bridge	13
罢了	bà le	merely	17	比富炫阔	bǐfù xuànkuò	flaunt one's wealth	2
白菜	báicài	Chinese cabbage, pak choi	11	◆ 比上不足，比下有余	bǐ shàng bùzú, bǐ xià yǒuyú	passable, tolerable	2
白粉	báifěn	white powder	13	笔挺	bǐtǐng	trim	2
白兰地	báilándì	brandy	2	弊	bì	disadvantage	5
百转回折	bǎizhuǎn huízhé	(of sound) making various changes in pitch, tune, etc.	13	必然	bìrán	neccesity	4
				编	biān	number, compile	1
摆	bǎi	lay, display	2	变化多端	biànhuà duōduān	change in various ways	6
◆ 扮相	bànxiàng	stage appearance	13	变奏	biànzòu	variation	4
伴奏	bànzòu	accompaniment	4	便于	biànyú	easy to	5
傍晚	bàngwǎn	dusk	2	辩证统一	biànzhèng tǒngyī	dialectical unity	4
包含	bāohán	include	13	标记	biāojì	mark, sign	3
保存	bǎocún	preserve	5	标志	biāozhì	symbol	9
饱览	bǎolǎn	feast one's eyes on something	6				

生词	拼音	译文	
标志性	biāozhìxìng	iconic	7
表演	biǎoyǎn	performance	13
别致	biézhì	unique and elegant	1
波动	bōdòng	fluctuate	11
补偿金	bǔcháng jīn	compensation	18

生词	拼音	译文	
布帛	bùbó	cloth and silk	15
布局	bùjú	layout	1
布娃娃	bùwáwa	cloth doll	15
部位	bùwèi	part	12

生词	拼音	译文	
裁	cái	cut	15
彩画	cǎihuà	colour painting	4
踩	cǎi	step on	12
苍蝇	cāngying	fly (insect)	3
操纵	cāozòng	control	15
◆ 曹雪芹	Cáo Xuěqín	Cao Xueqin (1715–1763), author of *The Dream of the Red Chamber*	14
策马奔腾	cèmǎ bēnténg	whipping and riding the horse	13
长裤	chángkù	trousers	2
◆ 《长生殿》	"Chángshēng Diàn"	*The Palace of Eternal Youth*	14
敞	chǎng	spacious, open	5
敞快	chǎngkuài	cheerful	5
唱述	chàngshù	tell a story by singing	15
◆ 朝房	cháofáng	reception room for officials (in former times)	4
◆ 朝政	cháozhèng	state affairs	15
尘寰	chénhuán	the universe, the world	11
衬衫	chènshān	shirt	2
撑船破浪	chēngchuán pòlàng	rolling the boat and breaking the waves	13
成就	chéngjiù	achievement	4

生词	拼音	译文	
◆ 成龙	Chéng Lóng	Jackie Chen, Chinese *Kung Fu* star	9
成书	chéngshū	be written	14
成为	chéngwéi	become	6
◆ 城楼	chénglóu	gate tower	3
城墙根下	chéngqiáng gēn xià	by the foot of the city wall	3
池子	chízi	pond	1
翅膀	chìbǎng	wing	11
重复	chóngfù	repetition	4
筹集	chóují	raise (funding)	8
◆ 丑角	chǒujué	comic, villainous or righteous characters in Beijing opera, recognised by the patch of white paint around the eyes and nose	13
出访	chūfǎng	visit a foreign country	8
出席	chūxí	attend	9
除去	chúqù	except	4
穿	chuān	wear	2
川流不息	chuānliú bùxī	ceaselessly move around as a flowing river	2
传递	chuándì	pass on	12
传教士	chuánjiàoshì	missionary	15
船桨	chuánjiǎng	roar	13

生词	拼音	译文	
创造	chuàngzào	create	10
创作	chuàngzuò	creation	4
啜	chuò	sip	2

生词	拼音	译文	
此后	cǐhòu	afterwards	10
从前	cóngqián	in the past	16

生词	拼音	译文	
达观	dáguān	optimistic	5
打击乐器	dǎjī yuèqì	percussion instruments	15
打听	dǎting	ask about	10
大半个	dà bàn ge	a greater half	2
大街小巷	dàjiē xiǎoxiàng	big streets and small alleys; all the streets in the area	3
◆ 大麦茶绿豆汤	dàmàichá lǜdòutāng	barley tea and mung bean soup	2
大同小异	dàtóng xiǎoyì	virtually the same	4
代表	dàibiǎo	represent	7
单调	dāndiào	monotonous	4
单体	dāntǐ	single	6
◆ 旦角	dànjué	female characters in Beijing opera	13
当成	dāngchéng	treat ... as ...	9
倒	dǎo	fall, collapse	3
◆ 倒笔架	dào bǐjià	inverted pen-rack	7
倒映	dàoyìng	reflect	15
灯光	dēngguāng	light	15
灯笼	dēnglong	lantern	11
滴溜溜	dīliūliū	motion of rolling or flowing	11
点出	diǎn chū	point out	6

生词	拼音	译文	
◆ 殿	diàn	hall	4
雕饰	diāoshì	carving	4
◆ 吊板桥	diàobǎn qiáo	hanging bridge	3
叠	dié	overlap, put one thing on top of another	12
碟	dié	dish	2
◆ 顶天立地	dǐngtiān lìdì	stand upright on one's own two legs between heaven and earth	5
鼎盛	dǐngshèng	at the height of prosperity	14
◆ 东城	Dōngchéng	Dongcheng District	11
◆ 东四南大街	Dōngsì Nán Dàjiē	Dongsi South Avenue	11
懂事	dǒngshì	intelligent	17
洞察	dòngchá	perceive	18
都市	dūshì	city	2
独霸	dúbà	dominate	14
独特	dútè	unique	6
笃	dǔ	kick the shuttlecock with the inner side of the heel of the right foot	12
◆ 端门	Duān Mén	Duan Gate	4
对称	duìchèn	symmetrical	1
◆ 对弈	duìyì	play go	10

E

生词	拼音	译文	
鹅毛	émáo	goose feather	12

生词	拼音	译文	
◆ 二郎庙	Èrláng Miào	Erlang Temple	11

F

生词	拼音	译文	
法国	Fǎguó	France	15
法律	fǎlǜ	law	18
帆布床	fānbù chuáng	camp bed	2
反复	fǎnfù	repetitive	7
范围	fànwéi	range	3
方方正正	fāngfāngzhèngzhèng	square-shaped	1
仿佛	fǎngfú	as if	11
分隔	fēngé	separate	6

生词	拼音	译文	
封闭式	fēngbìshì	closed	7
风范依存	fēngfàn yīcún	of past glamour	3
缝	féng	sew	12
俸禄	fènglù	salary	16
斧子	fǔzi	axe	10
俯瞰	fǔkàn	overlook	11
腐烂	fǔlàn	rot	10
复杂	fùzá	complex	10

G

生词	拼音	译文	
改造	gǎizào	reform, remake	15
干扰	gānrǎo	disturb	5
感谢	gǎnxiè	thank	18
高空	gāokōng	high in the sky	11
高头大马	gāotóu dàmǎ	tall horse	3
高雅脱俗	gāoyǎ tuōsú	graceful and distinguished	8
◆ 阁	gé	pavilion, cabinet	4
构成	gòuchéng	form	2
古称	gǔ chēng	be known in ancient times as	10
古城	gǔchéng	ancient city	3
古今中外	gǔjīn zhōngwài	in the past and the present, at home and abroad	4
古昔	gǔxī	antiquity	3

生词	拼音	译文	
拐	guǎi	turn, bend the right knee sideways and kick the shuttlecock with the outer side of the right foot	12
观阵	guān zhèn	observe a game of chess	10
官职	guānzhí	official position	16
观众	guānzhòng	spectator, audience	14
掼	guàn	toss	12
惯	guàn	be used to	1
光影	guāngyǐng	light and shadow	4
广泛	guǎngfàn	widely	10
广阔	guǎngkuò	vast	5
贵	guì	highly valued	5

生词	拼音	译文	
◆ 国粹	guócuì	quintessence of Chinese culture	13

生词	拼音	译文	
◆ 国服	guófú	national dress	8

H

生词	拼音	译文	
蛤蟆	háma	frog, toad	11
孩提	háití	childhood	11
◆《汉书》	"Hàn Shū"	*History of the Han Dynasty*, a dynastic history by Ban Gu (32–92)	15
◆ 汉武帝	Hàn Wǔdì	Emperor Wu of the Han Dynasty	15
豪情长啸	háoqíng chángxiào	let out a long cry of lofty ambitions	3
好莱坞	Hǎoláiwū	Hollywood	9
合	hé	closeness	5
赫然	hèrán	awesomely	3
轰动一时	hōngdòng yìshí	create a great sensation	15
◆《红楼梦》	"Hónglóu Mèng"	*The Dream of the Red Chamber*	14
红润	hóngrùn	ruddy	12

生词	拼音	译文	
后背	hòubèi	back	7
蝴蝶	húdié	butterfly	11
◆ 护城河	hùchéng hé	moat	3
◆ 花石门墩	huā shí méndūn	porphyry gate pier	3
花样	huāyàng	variety	12
◆ 华州	Huàzhōu	Huazhou District in Shaanxi Province	15
怀疑	huáiyí	doubt	3
环顾悠然	huángù yōurán	look around leisurely	2
缓解	huǎnjiě	alleviate	6
喤喤喤	huánghuáng huáng	an onomatopoeic word describing the sound of heavy vehicles passing by, vroom	3
浑厚	húnhòu	(of voice) resonant and deep	13
获得	huòdé	acquire, receive	18

J

生词	拼音	译文	
鸡毛	jīmáo	chicken feather	12
及于	jí yú	reach to	8
极少数	jí shǎoshù	few	4
集市	jíshì	marketplace	17
技术	jìshù	technique, skill	12
季节	jìjié	season	11
架	jià	prop up	6
监察	jiānchá	supervision	7

生词	拼音	译文	
◆ 剪辫易服	jiǎn biàn yì fú	the cutting of the "queue" (men's braid) and the change of clothing	7
剪影	jiǎnyǐng	silhouette	15
简单	jiǎndān	simple	12
间或	jiànhuò	occasionally, once in a while	12

生词	拼音	译文	
见微知著	jiànwēi zhīzhù	recognise the whole through observation of a small part	18
◆ 毽友	jiànyǒu	shuttlecock friends, people who play shuttlecock together	12
建筑物	jiànzhùwù	building	2
◆ 毽子	jiànzi	shuttlecock, a traditional Chinese game, in which players try to keep a weighted shuttlecock in the air by kicking	12
◆ 毽子托	jiànzi tuō	the weighted base of a shuttlecock	12
讲究	jiǎngjiu	refined	2
◆ 角楼	jiǎolóu	turret	3
教诲	jiàohuì	teaching	17
教育	jiàoyù	educate	17
接待	jiēdài	receive	8
阶级	jiējí	class, social stratum	11
接受	jiēshòu	accept	16
杰出	jiéchū	distinguished	4
结合	jiéhé	combine	6
解释	jiěshì	explain	9
届	jiè	when or which	2
斤斤计较	jīnjīn jìjiào	calculating and unwilling to make any sacrifice	5

生词	拼音	译文	
劲	jìn	strong	11
◆ 晋朝	Jìncháo	Jin Dynasty (265–420)	10
◆ 京剧	jīngjù	Beijing opera	13
惊人	jīngrén	astonishing	14
精髓	jīngsuí	essence	13
◆ 景山五亭	Jǐngshān wǔ tíng	five pavilions of Jingshan	6
景物	jǐngwù	scenery	6
◆ 净行	jìngháng	male characters with painted faces in Beijing opera, usually virile or with rough character	13
竞技	jìngjì	competition	10
竞争性	jìngzhēng xìng	competitiveness	5
静美	jìngměi	solemnly beautiful	13
境界	jìngjiè	realm	3
究竟	jiūjìng	exactly, on earth	10
久而久之	jiǔ'ér jiǔzhī	as time goes by	9
救	jiù	save	18
拘谨	jūjǐn	over-cautious	5
居住	jūzhù	live	5
居住者	jūzhùzhě	resident	5
举国若狂	jǔguó ruòkuáng	nationwide craze	14
具	jù	possess, have	3
剧本	jùběn	play script	14
剧坛	jùtán	the operatic world	14

生词	拼音	译文	
卡拉 OK	kǎlā ŌK	karaoke	14
开衩	kāichà	split, opening	8
开春	kāichūn	the beginning of spring	11

生词	拼音	译文	
砍柴	kǎnchái	cut down trees for firewood	10
考究	kǎojiu	exquisite	11
铿锵	kēngqiāng	with a strong beat	13

生词	拼音	译文	
口袋	kǒudai	pocket	7
扣子	kòuzi	button	7
枯燥	kūzào	dull	4
款	kuǎn	style	7
◆ 昆明湖	Kūnmíng Hú	Kunming Lake	6
◆ 昆曲	kūnqǔ	*kunqu*, opera using kunqiang melodies and popular in southern Jiangsu Province, Beijing, and Hebei Province	14

生词	拼音	译文	
◆ 昆曲清唱	kūnqǔ qīngchàng	the activity of singing kunqu without instrumental accompaniment	14
困难	kùnnan	difficulty	10

生词	拼音	译文	
落水者	luòshuǐ zhě	drowning person	18
蜡烛	làzhú	candle	15
◆ 烂柯	Lànkē	namely "rotting axe", another name for go	10
◆ 廊	láng	veranda	4
廊引人随	láng yǐn rén suí	the veranda leads people to walk along	6
◆ 礼义廉耻	lǐ yì lián chǐ	rite, righteousness, honesty and shame	7
立法	lìfǎ	legislation	7
立即	lìjí	immediately	3
利落	lìluo	agile	12
历时	lìshí	last; take (a period of time)	14
例外	lìwài	except for	4
莲蕖	liánqú	lotus	6
◆ 莲子百合红枣汤	liánzǐ bǎihé hóngzǎo tāng	lotus seed, lily root and Chinese-date soup	2
◆ 脸谱	liǎnpǔ	types of facial makeup indicating personalities and characters in Chinese operas	13

生词	拼音	译文	
两侧	liǎngcè	both sides	8
凌波漫步	língbō mànbù	walk over ripples	6
灵魂	línghún	soul	13
零乱	língluàn	messy	4
领取	lǐngqǔ	receive	18
流传	liúchuán	spread	14
龙井鱼	lóngjǐng yú	dragon-eyed goldfish	11
笼	lǒng	cover, enshroud	2
◆ 弄堂	lòngtáng	narrow lane or alley	2
◆ 鲁国	Lǔ Guó	State of Lu, one of the Warring States into which China was divided during the Eastern Zhou Period (770 BC–256 BC)	18
略施脂粉	lüèshī zhīfěn	with light make-up	13
沦为	lúnwéi	be reduced to	18
轮廓	lúnkuò	outline	4
轮流	lúnliú	take turns	12
◆ 锣鼓经	luógǔjīng	a tune played by percussion instruments	13

生词	拼音	译文	
马鞭	mǎbiān	horsewhip	13
漫步	mànbù	stroll	4
曼声	mànshēng	drawl	2
◆ 梅兰芳	Méi Lánfāng	Mei Lanfang (1894–1961), a famed Beijing opera artist	13
美人	měirén	beauty	11
魅力	mèilì	charm	3
门洞	méndòng	doorway, gateway	12
迷魂阵	míhúnzhèn	maze, labyrinth	2
迷路	mílù	get lost	1
面料	miànliào	fabric	7
面目皆非	miànmù jiē fēi	beyond recognition	10
面色	miànsè	complexion	12

生词	拼音	译文	
民间	mínjiān	folk	15
民权	mínquán	Principle of Democracy, civil rights	7
民生	mínshēng	Principle of the People's Livelihood	7
敏感	mǐngǎn	sensitive	5
名著	míngzhù	masterpiece	14
明快	míngkuài	light and cheerful	13
模样	múyàng	appearance, look	3
抹	mǒ	measure word for cloud, etc.	13
末期	mòqī	final phase	10
◆ 《牡丹亭》	"Mǔdān Tíng"	*The Peony Pavilion*	14
幕布	mùbù	curtain	15

生词	拼音	译文	
纳凉	nàliáng	enjoy the cool in hot weather	2
乃至	nǎizhì	and even	15
男装	nánzhuāng	man's suit	7
难于通行	nányú tōngxíng	difficult to go through	2
闹着玩儿	nàozhe wánr	say or do something as a joke	17

生词	拼音	译文	
◆ 内务部街	Nèiwùbù Jiē	Neiwubu Street	11
溺水者	nìshuǐzhě	drowning person	18
年代	niándài	era, year	10
鲇鱼	niányú	catfish	11
◆ 念白	niànbái	recitation, spoken parts in a Chinese opera	13
奴隶	núlì	slave	18

生词	拼音	译文	
欧洲	Ōuzhōu	Europe	15

生词	拼音	译文	
偶然	ǒurán	occasionally	11

生词	拼音	译文	
拍	pāi	shoot (a film)	9
排列有序	páiliè yǒuxù	orderly arranged	3
配合	pèihé	co-operation	12
疲劳	píláo	fatigue	6
◆ 皮影木偶	píyǐng mùǒu	shadow puppet	3
◆ 皮影戏	píyǐngxì	shadow puppetry	15
癖好	pǐhào	hobby, fetish	11

生词	拼音	译文	
偏爱	piān'ài	prefer	8
片场	piànchǎng	set	9
片刻	piànkè	a moment	6
颦	pín	frown	13
品行	pǐnxíng	moral conduct	18
铺	pù	shop	11

Q

生词	拼音	译文	
欺骗	qīpiàn	deceive	17
◆ 旗袍	qípáo	cheongsam	8
棋艺	qíyì	board game skill	10
起伏	qǐfú	undulating	13
起源	qǐyuán	originate	10
气派	qìpài	dignified air	3
气势磅礴	qìshì pángbó	of tremendous momentum	13
气质	qìzhì	temperament	5
千篇一律	qiānpiān yílù	stereotyped	4
◆ 前三殿	qián sān diàn	the First Three Halls of the Palace Museum, namely *Taihe Dian* (Hall of Supreme Harmony), *Zhonghe Dian* (Hall of Central Harmony), and *Baohe Dian* (Hall of Preserving Harmony)	4
前瞻后顾	qiánzhān hòugù	look forward and backward, look around	4

生词	拼音	译文	
◆ 乾嘉（年号）	QiánJiā (niánhào)	1736–1820, Qing Dynasty reign titles (Qianlong and Jiaqing)	14
◆ 乾隆（年号）	Qiánlóng (niánhào)	1736–1795, Qing Dynasty reign title	14
◆ 腔	qiāng	melodies for the singing part in a Chinese opera	13
瞧	qiáo	look	1
怯懦	qiènuò	timid and overcautious	3
◆ 秦腔	qínqiāng	Qinqiang Opera, a folk Chinese opera originated in Shaanxi, China	3
青年	qīngnián	youth	10
青苔	qīngtái	green moss	3
轻盈	qīngyíng	light	6
◆ 清廉为官	qīnglián wéiguān	work as a government official free of corruption	16
蜻蜓	qīngtíng	dragonfly	11

生词	拼音	译文	
情趣	qíngqù	joy	11
情致	qíngzhì	emotion	5
请教	qǐngjiào	consult	10
区别	qūbié	distinguish	7
曲折	qūzhé	meandering	5

生词	拼音	译文	
◆ 衢州市	Qúzhōu shì	Quzhou City in Zhejiang Province	10
取得	qǔdé	achieve	4
去世	qùshì	pass away	15
诠释	quánshì	interpret	13
缺少	quēshǎo	lack	5

生词	拼音	译文	
然而	rán'ér	however	2
冉冉上升	rǎnrǎn shàngshēng	rise gradually	11
热闹非凡	rènao fēifán	extraordinarily bustling	14

生词	拼音	译文	
人家	rénjia	other people	9
人情	rénqíng	human emotions	18
忍不住	rěnbuzhù	cannot help but	3
容易	róngyì	easy	4
如此	rúcǐ	so, such	10

生词	拼音	译文	
◆ 三民主义	Sānmín Zhǔyì	"Three People's Principles" (Nationalism, Democracy and People's Livelihood, as put forward by Dr. Sun Yat-Sen)	7
◆ 三权分立	Sānquán Fēnlì	Separation of (the Three) Powers	7
散漫	sǎnmàn	unorganised	4
色彩	sècǎi	colour	15
杀	shā	kill	17
沙燕	shāyàn	bank swallow	11
山洞	shāndòng	mountain cave	10
上演	shàngyǎn	enact	3

生词	拼音	译文	
上衣	shàngyī	top	7
设计	shèjì	design	1
身板	shēnbǎn	body, figure	12
◆ 身段	shēnduàn	the graceful bearing of opera performers	13
深厚	shēnhòu	deep	5
深色调	shēn sèdiào	dark tones	8
神采	shéncǎi	elegant demeanour	13
神情恍惚	shénqíng huǎnghū	in a trance	15
神韵	shényùn	charm	13
生病	shēngbìng	get sick	15
◆ 生角	shēngjué	male characters in Beijing opera	13
盛行	shèngxíng	prevail	14

生词	拼音	译文	
失去	shīqù	lose	16
◆ 诗境	shījìng	the realm of poetry	5
诗情画意	shīqíng huàyì	poetic beauty	6
◆ 十七孔长桥	Shíqīkǒng Chángqiáo	Seventeen-Arch Bridge	6
◆ 石雀胡同	Shíquè Hútòng	Shique *Hutong*, Stone Sparrow Hutong	1
时而	shí'ér	once in a while	2
时期	shíqī	era, period	10
实在	shízài	truly, virtually	18
◆ 史家胡同	Shǐjiā Hútòng	Shijia Hutong	11
始终	shǐzhōng	from the beginning to the end	2
市井小民	shìjǐng xiǎomín	plebeians	14
饰演	shìyǎn	play the role of ...	9
视野	shìyě	vision	5
收集	shōují	collect	3
首都	shǒudū	capital	6
手段	shǒuduàn	method	4
手卷	shǒujuàn	hand scroll	4
受困	shòukùn	be trapped	18
兽皮	shòupí	leather	15
舒展	shūzhǎn	extend	5
赎	shú	ransom	18
◆ 术士	shùshì	alchemist	15
◆ 水袖	shuǐxiù	water sleeves, double white silk sleeves attached to the cuffs of traditional Chinese	

生词	拼音	译文	
		opera or dance costumes	13
◆ 舜	Shùn	Emperor Shun, legendary sage-king in remote antiquity of China	10
司法	sīfǎ	jurisdiction	7
思念心切	sīniàn xīnqiè	painfully miss someone	15
四顾环绕	sìgù huánrào	connected on the four sides	5
◆ 四合院	sìhéyuàn	Siheyuan, Chinese courtyard	3
四周	sìzhōu	all around, on all sides	6
似乎	sìhū	seemingly	5
◆ 宋霭龄	Sòng Ǎilíng	Soong Eling	8
◆ 宋美龄	Sòng Měilíng	Soong May-Ling	8
◆ 宋庆龄	Sòng Qìnglíng	Soong Ching-Ling	8
◆ 宋氏三姐妹	Sòngshì sān jiěmèi	Three Sisters of the Soong Family	8
俗称	súchēng	generally known as	13
素雅	sùyǎ	simple but elegant	8
素养	sùyǎng	personal quality	5
岁时	suìshí	seasons and time of the year	5
◆ 碎步	suìbù	a special motion in Beijing opera, to walk with short quick steps	13
损伤	sǔnshāng	harm	18

生词	拼音	译文	
坛	tán	altar	1
坦然	tǎnrán	honest	5

生词	拼音	译文	
◆ 唐装	tángzhuāng	Tang suit	9

生词	拼音	译文	
◆《桃花扇》	"Táohuā Shàn"	*The Peach Blossom Fan*	14
特点	tèdiǎn	feature	8
藤椅	téngyǐ	cane chair	2
踢法	tīfǎ	kicking technique	12
◆ 天、地、日、月坛	Tiān, Dì, Rì, YuèTán	Temple of Heaven, Temple of the Earth, Temple of the Sun and Temple of the Moon	1
条件	tiáojiàn	condition	5
贴水而过	tiē shuǐ ér guò	sweep past water	6
◆ 庭院深深深几许	tíngyuàn shēnshēn shēn jǐ xǔ	Deep, deep is the courtyard.	5

生词	拼音	译文	
同胞	tóngbāo	compatriot	18
童子	tóngzǐ	young lad	10
偷	tōu	stand on one foot and kick the shuttlecock with the other foot behind the body	12
头条	tóu tiáo	(used in *hutong* names) the First *Hutong*	1
突然	tūrán	suddenly	3
涂	tú	colour, paint	15
腿脚	tuǐjiǎo	leg and foot, ability to walk	12

生词	拼音	译文	
外宾	wàibīn	foreign guest	8
◆ 外省	wài shěng	provinces other than where one is	1
玩耍	wánshuǎ	play, have fun	15
完整	wánzhěng	complete	3
宛如	wǎnrú	as if	6
婉约	wǎnyuē	graceful	6
◆ 万历（年号）	Wànlì (niánhào)	1573–1620, Ming Dynasty reign	14
王卿贵族	wángqīng guìzú	aristocrats	14
往往	wǎngwǎng	often	4
望其项背	wàngqí xiàngbèi	capable of catching up with sb	14
微弱	wēiruò	weak	11
◆ 围棋	wéiqí	go, a type of board game played with black and white pieces on a square wooden board	10

生词	拼音	译文	
尾巴	wěiba	tail	11
娓娓念唱	wěiwěi niànchàng	recite and sing opera lines elegantly and tirelessly	13
文学经典	wénxué jīngdiǎn	literature classic	14
稳	wěn	stable	11
卧波	wòbō	(figurative use of bridges) lie on the waves	6
无数	wúshù	countless	4
蜈蚣	wúgōng	centipede	11
◆ 午门	Wǔ Mén	the Meridian Gate	4
◆ 庑	wǔ	side room	4

X

生词	拼音	译文	
膝盖	xīgài	knee	8
西斜	xī xié	(of the sun) set in the west	10
吸引	xīyǐn	attract	6
喜怒哀乐	xǐnù āilè	joy, anger, sorrow and happiness; all emotions	13
弦乐	xiányuè	string instruments	15
显著	xiǎnzhù	distinctive	8
◆ 香饵胡同	Xiāng'ěr Hútòng	Xiang'er *Hutong*, Delicious Bait Hutong	1
◆ 香影廊	Xiāngyǐng Láng	Xiangying Veranda	6
消暑祛疫	xiāoshǔ qūyì	reduce heat and curb diseases	2
小板凳	xiǎo bǎndèng	small stool	2
小翻领	xiǎo fānlǐng	narrow turn-down collar	7

生词	拼音	译文	
◆ 小花脸	xiǎo huāliǎn	another name for *chou* characters	13
小憩	xiǎoqì	take a short rest	6
◆ 小钱	xiǎo qián	holed copper coin	12
效果	xiàoguǒ	effect	4
斜	xié	inclining	1
◆ 辛亥革命	Xīnhài Gémìng	Revolution of 1911	7
新式礼服	xīnshì lǐfú	new-style suit	7
形成	xíngchéng	form	7
形式	xíngshì	form	6
形形色色	xíngxíngsèsè	of all forms	11
行政	xíngzhèng	administration	7
凶猛	xiōngměng	ferocious	11
修改	xiūgǎi	modify	7
袖口	xiùkǒu	cuff	7
虚化	xūhuà	virtual	13
栩栩如生	xǔxǔ rú shēng	vivid	15

Y

生词	拼音	译文	
◆ 雅部	yǎ bù	the refined opera, another name for *kunqu*	14
雅洁精巧	yǎjié jīngqiǎo	elegant and exquisite	6
雅俗共赏	yǎsú-gòngshǎng	appealing to both refined and popular tastes	14
◆ 烟袋斜街	Yāndài Xiéjiē	Yandai Xiejie, Inclining Pipe Street	1
严冬	yándōng	severe winter	11
炎雾	yánwù	summer heat	2

生词	拼音	译文	
眼前	yǎnqián	in front of one's eyes	3
演员	yǎnyuán	actor, actress	9
扬	yáng	throw up, kick the shuttlecock with the toes of the right foot	12
仰观	yǎngguān	look up	3
样式	yàngshì	design	7
◆ 尧	Yáo	Emperor Yao, legendary sage-king in remote antiquity of China	10

生词	拼音	译文	
遥远	yáoyuǎn	remote	3
一辈子	yíbèizi	all one's life, a life	16
◆ 一场愁梦 酒醒时， 斜阳却照 深深院	yì chǎng chóu mèng jiǔ xǐng shí, xiéyáng què zhào shēnshēn yuàn	When I woke up from a sad dream, the setting sun was shining on the deep courtyard.	5
一截	yì jié	a length of	12
一体	yìtǐ	unity	10
依靠	yīkào	rely on	6
移步幻影	yí bù huàn yǐng	(of scenery) change with each step	6
◆ 颐和园	Yíhé Yuán	the Summer Palace	6
怡然自得	yírán zìdé	enjoy oneself	11
以…… 取胜	yǐ... qǔ shèng	win out by ...	6
以至	yǐzhì	so much so (that...)	3
艺术	yìshù	art	3
艺坛	yìtán	the world of art	15
◆ 弈	yì	the ancient name of go	10
意境	yìjìng	artistic concept	13
意味深长	yìwèi shēncháng	with profundity	13
音乐	yīnyuè	music	14
◆ 银耳羹	yín'ěrgēng	white fungus soup	2
◆ 樱桃斜街	Yīngtao Xiéjiē	Yingtao Xiejie, Inclining Cherry Street	1
影响力	yǐngxiǎnglì	influence	8

生词	拼音	译文	
影像	yǐngxiàng	image	15
影子	yǐngzi	shadow	15
永远	yǒngyuǎn	forever	9
勇于	yǒngyú	be brave to	18
优雅	yōuyǎ	elegant	13
游览线	yóulǎn xiàn	sight-seeing route	6
游鳞	yóu lín	swimming fish	6
游山玩水	yóushān wánshuǐ	travel to mountains and rivers, travel extensively	11
游戏	yóuxì	game	11
◆ 有藏有露	yǒucáng yǒulòu	covering some while showing others	5
有闲	yǒu xián	(of people) have much leisure time, not occupied by work	11
黝黑如铁	yǒuhēi rútiě	dark as iron	3
羽扇	yǔshàn	feather fan	2
渊源	yuānyuán	origin	15
原始社会	yuánshǐ shèhuì	primitive society	10
远走高飞	yuǎnzǒu gāofēi	travel to faraway places	11
◆ 月到风 来亭	Yuèdào Fēnglái Tíng	Yuedao Fenglai Pavilion	6
乐曲	yuèqǔ	music	4
◆ 芸芸众生	yúnyún zhòngshēng	the masses	2
运动量	yùndòng liàng	amount of physical exercise	12
韵味	yùnwèi	style	13

生词	拼音	译文	
◆ 宰相	zǎixiàng	premiere, chancellor	16

生词	拼音	译文	
在于	zàiyú	lie in	5

生词	拼音	译文	
则	zé	so, thus, therefore	1
增添	zēngtiān	add to	6
◆ 曾子	Zēngzǐ	Zengzi (505 BC–436 BC), Chinese philosopher	17
赠送	zèngsòng	give	16
展示	zhǎnshì	display	6
照射	zhàoshè	light up	15
遮挡	zhēdǎng	cover	15
◆ 浙江省	Zhèjiāng shěng	Zhejiang Province	10
整体	zhěngtǐ	unity	6
正确	zhèngquè	correct	17
正是	zhèngshì	exactly	8
◆ 郑国	Zhèngguó	Zheng state	16
◆ 郑相却鱼	Zhèng xiàng què yú	the Premier of Zheng refuses the gift of fish	16
职业演员	zhíyè yǎnyuán	professional actor	14
纸板	zhǐbǎn	cardboard	15
制止	zhìzhǐ	stop	17
置身（于）	zhìshēn (yú)	place oneself (in)	4
忠奸善恶	zhōngjiān shàn'è	the loyal, the treacherous, the good and the evil; all kinds of people	13
◆ 钟、鼓楼	Zhōng, Gǔ Lóu	Bell Tower and Drum Tower	1
中心	zhōngxīn	centre	1
种类繁多	zhǒnglèi fánduō	various, diverse	11
重施油彩	zhòngshī yóucǎi	with heavy make-up	13
周围	zhōuwéi	surrounding	4
猪	zhū	pig	17
逐步	zhúbù	gradually	17
竹榻	zhútà	bamboo couch	2
煮	zhǔ	boil	17
主题	zhǔtí	theme	4
著名	zhùmíng	famous	8
抓	zhuā	catch	17
◆ 砖雕门楼	zhuān diāo ménlóu	gate house with carved bricks	3
转向	zhuànxiàng	lose one's sense of direction	1
撞衫	zhuàngshān	accidentally wear the same clothes	9
坠入	zhuìrù	fall into	3
准备	zhǔnbèi	prepare	17
着装	zhuózhuāng	clothing	8
资金	zījīn	funding	8
姿势	zīshì	posture	12
◆ 子贡	Zǐgòng	Zigong, student of Confucius	18
◆ 子路	Zǐlù	Zilu, student of Confucius	18
◆ 紫禁城	Zǐjìnchéng	the Forbidden City	1
自成一统	zìchéng yìtǒng	unique in its own system	5
自然界	zìránjiè	nature	5
总是	zǒngshì	always	1
纵（的）	zòng (de)	vertical	2
组合	zǔhé	integrate	6
组群	zǔqún	group	4
左睇右盼	zuǒdì yòupàn	look to the left and right, look around	4
◆ 坐井观天	zuòjǐng guāntiān	view the sky from the bottom of the well	5
作品	zuòpǐn	work	4
作用	zuòyòng	effect	6

郑重声明

读者意见反馈

为收集对教材的意见建议,进一步完善教材编写并做好服务工作,读者可将对本教材的意见建议通过如下渠道反馈至我社。

咨询电话　0086-10-58581350
反馈邮箱　xp@hep.com.cn
通信地址　北京市西城区德外大街4号
　　　　　高等教育出版社海外出版事业部（国际语言文化出版中心）
邮政编码　100120